Old and New

OLD AND NEW

Jesus' Seven Parables of the Kingdom
(Matthew 13)

MARTIN EMMRICH

WIPF & STOCK · Eugene, Oregon

OLD AND NEW
Jesus' Seven Parables of the Kingdom (Matthew 13)

Copyright © 2022 Martin Emmrich. All rights reserved. Except for brief quotations in critical publications or reviews, no part of this book may be reproduced in any manner without prior written permission from the publisher. Write: Permissions, Wipf and Stock Publishers, 199 W. 8th Ave., Suite 3, Eugene, OR 97401.

Wipf & Stock
An Imprint of Wipf and Stock Publishers
199 W. 8th Ave., Suite 3
Eugene, OR 97401

www.wipfandstock.com

PAPERBACK ISBN: 978-1-6667-3168-2
HARDCOVER ISBN: 978-1-6667-2440-0
EBOOK ISBN: 978-1-6667-2441-7

JANUARY 5, 2022 8:35 AM

Scripture quotations are from the ESV (English Standard Version), copyright 2001 by Crossway, a publishing ministry of Good News Publishers. All rights reserved.

Contents

Preface | *vii*

Introduction | 1

1 The Kingdom Requires a Decision | 12

2 The Kingdom as God's Decision | 27

3 The Kingdom Admits of Opposition | 36

4 The Kingdom's Humble Seed and Miraculous Growth | 46

5 The Kingdom's Hidden Growth | 57

6 The Kingdom Revealed in Its Full Expression | 67

7 The Kingdom's Inestimable Value | 75

8 The Kingdom Asserts Universal Claim | 85

9 Old and New in Perspective | 92

Bibliography | *103*

Preface

THE IDEA FOR *OLD AND New* came to me while I was reviewing a sermon manuscript submitted by an intern at Westminster Presbyterian Church. The sermon was on a parable from Matthew 13. As I turned to briefly look at the chapter, I began to see several details that I had never noticed before. Lights went on that arrested my interest. Over time, I kept pondering the seven parables of the kingdom, until the idea for the present book formed in my mind. The raw division into a total of ten chapters, including the introduction and conclusion, followed soon after that.

In August of 2017, I had the opportunity to teach a course on Matthew 13 at the Reformiertes Theologisches Seminar (RTS) in Heidelberg, Germany. The feedback of the students further helped to crystallize the shape of the book. I sincerely hope that the finished product will not only aid in leading to a deeper understanding of this skillfully arranged, magnificent chapter in Matthew's Gospel, but afford a window into how Jesus himself thought of the kingdom that he had come to proclaim. It is for this purpose, so I believe, that Matthew created the collection of parables. But when all is said and done, my ambition is above all to encourage and edify Christ's disciples, whom he calls his "scribes" (Matt 13:52). After all, "All Scripture is breathed out by God and profitable for teaching, for reproof, for correction, and for training in righteousness," to equip all of his saints for every good work of the kingdom (2 Tim 3:16–17).

Introduction

"In six days the LORD made heaven and earth" (Exod 20:11). It took Jesus three days to lay the foundation for the redemption of the universe and the kingdom of God. But we need longer to see and believe it. God's good news of peace in Christ is seeping slowly through the rock of our hearts until the wonder breaks in us. "Behold, the kingdom of God is among you" (Luke 17:21). Jesus' contemporaries had waited for the coming of the kingdom of God. They had longed for the kingdom. They had prayed for it, researched, made calculations, and speculated about it—and they tragically missed it! It stood right in front of them, in the person of Jesus, and they failed to see it. How in all the world could this have happened?

The kingdom had arrived like a Swiss train on schedule, but it came to them completely differently than they had anticipated. Who could possibly conceive that God would become man? Then, having assumed human nature, the person of Jesus remained elusive and resisted the many attempts of people to figure him out, put him in a box, or predict his next move. He was so much like us that he could be mistaken for someone else, and yet "God was in Christ reconciling the world to himself" (2 Cor 5:19), a mystery if ever there was one. In a way, the advent of God's reign in the person of Christ was like an elaborate, grand play in a theater. The plot unfolds on the open stage, watched by all the spectators. But at the same time, there is something behind, under, or beside the stage, something which is unseen by the audience. In the world

OLD AND NEW

of the director, the lighting technicians, and sound engineers, a different kind of performance is unfurled. So it was with God who was present in Jesus, pulling the strings, but he could not be seen. What the eye-witnesses did see was the figure of a man from Galilee who could surprise them, offend them, convict and assure them, a miracle worker, but in the end, "he had no form or majesty... no beauty" (Isa 53:3) that anyone would see and desire him in truth. Indeed, he became "as one from whom men hide their faces, he was despised, and we esteemed him not" (53:3). So they missed the kingdom.

The teaching ministry of Jesus was destined to complete the paradox. His memorable stories about the kingdom were accessible even for children and the simplest of folks, which is why they heard him gladly. But although his stories revealed the nature of God's reign that now had reached its crucial phase, his teachings also served to conceal God's truth (cf. Matt 13:11). The kingdom as a "secret" (mystery) is intimately related to his habit of using parables. The present work is dedicated to Matthew's account of Jesus' parables of the kingdom, compiled in a most fascinating collection in chapter 13 of his Gospel, the go-to text for anyone who wishes to gain a grip on this unique kind of stories.

Matthew 13:1–52 contains seven kingdom parables. The passage in its present shape forms the third of Matthew's five great teaching discourses and is located near the center of the Gospel.[1] Although Matthew includes additional parables of Jesus (18:10–14, 21–35; 20:1–16; 21:28–32, 33–44; 22:1–14; 25:1–13, 14–30, 31–46), it is clear from the outset that the conspicuous concentration of the seven stories about the kingdom is intended as a representative selection. What did Jesus think about the kingdom of God? What did he see as its most salient characteristics? Matthew 13 is the benchmark of his signature teaching in parables. With full

---

1. Each of the five discourses is marked by the stereotypical formula, "And when Jesus had finished (these sayings/words/parables)..." The phrase occurs in 7:28; 11:1; 13:53; 19:1; 26:1.

Introduction

entitlement, Pennington calls this chapter "the one-stop shop" for understanding Jesus' kingdom parables.[2]

A quick glance at the context of Matthew 13 reveals that the highly concentrated collection is placed at a crucial junction in Matthew's narrative. Chapter 12 records the first high point of a simmering opposition to Jesus with the ominous Beelzebul controversy. Jesus healed a demoniac (12:22), only to be charged by the religious leaders of being under the sway of satanic power. The accusation is shown to be absurd and ludicrous, but the so-called blasphemy against the Holy Spirit also constitutes the height of rebellion and a sin that, unlike any other, will not be forgiven (12:31–32).[3] Jesus then continues to comment on the conflict with his teaching of the good and the bad tree (12:33–37), both of them known by their corresponding fruit. As the chapter draws to a close, repeated references to the looming final judgment against Jesus' enemies gather clout (12:37, 41, 42). Finally, the ominous teaching of the return of the unclean spirit (12:43–45) shows Jesus' opponents as the ones under the control of dark powers—a stunning turnaround.[4] If they remain so, they will not have a part in God's kingdom. The chapter concludes with a razor-sharp definition of the true family of Jesus, consisting only of those who keep his word (12:46–49)—how many of us evangelical Christians can live with it? The "circle of trust" implies a decision that is before all who hear Jesus, namely either to trust and obey him or not. The table is set for the discourse of chapter 13. This turning point in the Gospel, drawing the lines between Jesus and the people who will

---

2. Pennington, "Matthew 13," 14.

3. It is clear from context that the blasphemy against the Holy Spirit can only be committed by religious people who have come into contact with Jesus, either personally or through the record of his teachings, whose worldview also includes the active presence of the biblical character of Satan, the chief antagonist of God's plan of redemption. In other words, these are people who have adopted many biblical truths, but in the end attribute Jesus' power to demonic activity.

4. They are called "this evil generation" (12:45) and thereby identified as the targets of the analogy of the house haunted by demons.

eventually advocate his crucifixion,[5] prepares the reader for the stark dualism of the seven parables of the kingdom and the looming final separation of good and evil (cf. 13:40–43, 49–50). The separation that will be final is occurring already in the way people respond to Jesus and his message. Seen through this lens, Matthew 13 serves the function of a theological explanation of the "mixed reception"[6] of Jesus and what will come of it. This existential reality confronts us today no less in the words of Jesus.

Matthew 13 with its seven parables is also a highly structured text unit. There is certainly more than one way to "fly over" the material.[7] However, the view taken here suggests a fairly symmetrical arrangement of the stories in a 3-1-3 pattern. The first triad of parables all have a common theme in seed that is sown in a field or garden-like setting and in growth, even if unanticipated. Their common denominator thus lies in consistent agrarian images. There is also an intriguing trajectory of declining numbers observable in the trio. The parable of the sower features four types of soils, followed by the parable of the weeds, narrowing the scenario to only two kinds of plants that grow from seeds sown in the field, while the last of the three (mustard seed) deals with a single seed of minute size. The numerical trajectory is 4-2-1, with the last of the three stories providing a singular focus on the kingdom of heaven beyond the more complex settings of the previous two.

The fourth parable performs an interlocking function, like a hinge, in that it connects with both the first as well as the second triad of stories. Its link with the parable of the mustard seed, as a parable of growth, is obvious and thus forms a bridge to the first set of three.[8] At the same time, the parable of the leaven also shares

---

5. Notice, too, that 12:14 contains the first reference to the Pharisees plotting "how to destroy him." Chapter 12 casts a long shadow to the cross, where the scheming of the leaders will finally come to fruition.

6. Pennington, "Matthew 13," 17.

7. Pennington, "Matthew 13," 17, for a brief discussion of various approaches.

8. Their position adjacent to each other already suggests their affinity in the same way as this is the case with the parables of the hidden treasure and the precious pearl in the second triadic complex (13:44–46).

Introduction

important themes with parables five through seven. For one, its setting is domestic, which chimes well with the rest of the stories in that division, relating either to domestic life or to the world of commerce, with the agrarian context completely dropping from view in the second half of the chapter. Moreover, just as the leaven echoes the theme of growth contained in its immediate "neighbor" (mustard seed) on one side, so the hiding of the leaven in the flour prepares the reader for the hiding of the treasure in the first parable of the second set of three, the leaven's neighbor on the other side of the hinge. As for the closing three parables, it is remarkable that they too possess a harmonious common theme of worth or value judgments. More formal observations will be afforded in the course of the following chapters of this work, but at this point we may say that the arrangement is far from accidental. In fact, the organization of the seven stories in a 3-1-3 pattern should be viewed as the consequence of very purposeful and intentional redaction on Matthew's part.

The Sower

    The Weeds

        The Mustard Seed

            The Leaven

        The Treasure

    The Pearl

The Dragnet

The author pursued a plan precipitating in purposeful arrangement, and an initial clue is found in the extremities of the discourse, as a quick glance at the beginning and the end shows. The first parable portrays a scattering motion, as seed is sown virtually everywhere without discrimination. This *centrifugal*

OLD AND NEW

motion is counterbalanced in the last parable of the dragnet with *centripetal* force: fish or aquatic creatures of every possible kind are drawn into the net, again without discrimination. The opposing motions (*outwards* and *inwards*) describe how the kingdom *begins* to reveal itself (sower) and how it will be manifest in the *conclusion* of the age (dragnet). In both cases, however, the motions have notable corresponding features in their universal appeal: the sowing of seed everywhere and the gathering of creatures of every kind.[9]

Beyond these structural and thematic considerations, the discourse itself is punctured by three distinct sayings about the nature of the parables, which are planted like flags in well-measured distance or intervals. The first is located at the beginning (13:1–17), the second halfway through (13:34–35), and the third at the very conclusion (13:51–52) of the textual complex. All three emphasize the revelation of formerly hidden things, and as such furnish a critical hermeneutical key for the entire discourse. The closing words of Jesus to his disciples are particularly striking:

> "Have you understood these things?" They said to him, "Yes." And he said to them, "Therefore, every scribe who has been trained for the kingdom of heaven is like a master of a house, who brings out of his treasure what is new and what is old." (Matt 13:51–52)

In Jesus' own mind, his parables contained "what is new and what is old." A proper reading of the text unit, then, will have to begin with the question, "What is new about these parables?" How or in what ways do Jesus' stories go beyond the horizon of Old Testament revelation (i.e., "what is old")?[10]

Parables *per se* were not unheard of in the Old Testament Scriptures, nor in rabbinic instruction during the first century AD.[11] Although Jesus placed a high premium on this didactic

---

9. A fuller account of this will be offered in chapter 1.

10. This question will indeed be raised at various junctions throughout this work.

11. There are a few parables in the Old Testament prophets (for example, Isa 5:1–7) that Witherington sees as "a modification or extension of wisdom speech," cf. Witherington, *Jesus the Sage*, 183. As for rabbinic teachings at the

INTRODUCTION

style, it is not primarily the *frequency* of parables deployed in his speeches that sets his teaching apart. It is easy to miss the simple point that his parables were about the kingdom of God, something that is unique, or, shall we say, "new," to his treasury of stories. Rabbinic parables and similitudes were in essence moral tales with little or no appeal to the grand narrative of God's plan of redemption. Jesus' parables, on the other hand, derived their very *raison d'être* from the fact that God's dealings with his people were about to enter a new principal epoch, history had reached its high noon, the fullness of time, in Jesus' ministry (cf. Gal 4:4). Therefore, before we can identify any other novel elements in his parabolic instruction, it is this singular feature that must be considered first by way of introduction.

The parables are stories about God's kingdom, or, as Matthew prefers, "the kingdom of heaven."[12] Aside from the formula "The kingdom of heaven is like..." (Matt 13:24, 31, 33, 44, 45, 47), which serves as introduction to six of the seven parables in 13:1–52 with only minor variations, the term "kingdom" (*basileia*) is used no fewer than twelve times in our discourse. Like a lighthouse emitting a strong signal, this emphasis is rooted in Jesus' own style of instruction, the memory of which has been preserved by all three Synoptic accounts of Jesus' ministry. One cannot ignore the fact that the parables uniquely reflect Jesus' thinking about God's heavenly kingdom.

The uniqueness of Jesus' focus here is thrown into sharp relief by comparison with the rest of the New Testament documents. While Jesus simply cannot stop talking about the kingdom in the Synoptic Gospels, the term is used not only far less frequently in the remaining apostolic writings of the New Testament,[13] but

---

time of Jesus, they certainly included parabolic discourses, even though the rabbinic parables differed significantly in content, less so in form. For a discussion on rabbinic parables, see Young, *Jesus and His Jewish Parables*, 236–52.

12. The difference between the two phrases is merely stylistic.

13. John saw no need to reproduce the common emphasis of the Synoptic Gospels on this point. Though he knew that the other evangelists preserved an important characteristic of Jesus' teachings, he wanted his account to provide a different perspective on the life and work of Jesus and purposefully omitted

must be sought diligently to be found. Jesus' stress on the kingdom is even more striking when approached from an Old Testament angle. To be sure, Israel was a monarchy, and the concept of a kingdom of Israel was therefore well-known. However, the stereotypical phrase "kingdom of God/heaven" is never employed in the Old Testament. The royal psalms certainly broach the concept by looking forward to a worldwide dominion of God and of his anointed king (Pss 2; 45; 72). They also affirm Yahweh's supreme rule over all creation (Pss 96; 97), but the realization of the anticipated kingdom had to wait until another day in the distant future.

Finally, this distant future is broached in Daniel 2, with its apocalyptic language of God setting up his kingdom in the context of concrete historical, political events, uniquely putting the coming of God's anticipated rule on the "timeline." In Nebuchadnezzar's dream, a succession of four empires, culminating in the Roman Empire (2:40), gives way to another kingdom: "And in the days of those kings the God of heaven will set up a kingdom that shall never be destroyed, nor shall the kingdom be left to another people . . . it shall stand forever" (2:44). The notion of God's everlasting realm is reiterated in Daniel 6:26, and in Daniel's vision of the four beasts, in which the kingdom is finally identified as one that will be given to the "one like a son of man" (7:13), "and to him was given dominion and glory and a kingdom, that all peoples, nations, and languages should serve him; his dominion is an everlasting dominion, which shall not pass away, and his kingdom one that shall not be destroyed" (7:14).[14]

It is from Daniel 7 that Jesus derived his identity as the "Son of Man," a title that he took to himself as being conscious of fulfilling Daniel's vision. Indeed, if Jesus' unrelenting emphasis on the kingdom of God is unique, the title "Son of Man" is downright exclusive to the Gospels, and virtually disappears in Acts and the

references to the kingdom of God, except for a total of six. But a quick glance at the rest of the New Testament writings shows that the term "kingdom" loses the appeal that it has in the teachings of Jesus, as recorded in Matthew, Mark, and Luke.

14. In the second part of the vision, the angelic interpreter then also affirms that the same kingdom belongs to "the saints of the Most High" (Dan 7:27).

Introduction

epistles of the New Testament. But Jesus used this title of himself to avoid the political fallout of openly proclaiming himself the promised "son of David" and king before his time had come.

Israel's hopes certainly were pinned on the revival of the Davidic dynasty and "the offspring of David" (2 Sam 7:12–16; cf. Acts 1:6) in accord with several Old Testament promises (Gen 49:9–10; Num 24:17; Isa 9:6–7; 11:1–5; Mic 5:2, etc.) and the structure of biblical revelation as a whole. After all, since the beginning, when God had made himself known to father Abram (Gen 12:1–3; 15:7–20; 17:1–8), his promise consisted of three basic strands: There would be a people, a land, and also a king (cf. Gen 17:6) to rule over people and land. Israel at the time of Jesus was waiting for this king, whose coming would somehow coincide with their redemption.

As these three concepts traveled through time and took shape by subsequent divine revelations, they were also fulfilled in preliminary stages. By the time Israel moved out of Egypt, the promise of a nation had finally been fulfilled. God's covenant at Mt. Sinai formalized Israel's role as the nation of God, teaching them how to live in a unique relation to Yahweh, the God of the covenant. Then, after forty years in the wilderness, the covenant was renewed in the plains of Moab on the edge of Canaan, with the focal point being Israel's imminent life in the promised land. The whole book of Deuteronomy is the enshrinement of this covenant and was designed to prepare the people for the fulfillment of God's land promise upon the conquest of Canaan. No longer a nomadic people, Israel would face new circumstances in their daily existence in the land. So, the covenant that Moses made with the people in Moab was uniquely tailored to structure their sedentary life in Canaan with a permanent place of worship and a theocratic system of law and order. This system of law and order also included a human king of the tribe of Judah, as had been augured from the beginning (cf. Gen 49:9–10; Deut 17:14–20), although God always remained the true king of Israel.

After the abortive tenure of Saul, God moved to appoint David as king and promised that a son of David would eventually establish an everlasting kingdom, the kingdom of God (2 Sam 7:12–16). In his own time, the king would form a new people of God, beginning with a remnant from Israel but also including the gentile nations, who would share in the king's worldwide dominion and so eventually fulfill all of God's cosmic design (cf. Isa 49:6; Rev 11:15–18). Thus, the trajectory of God's Old Testament preliminary stages of fulfillment was *people, land,* and *king,* in this order. The coming of Christ as the promised king of David's line was the first and crucial step in the direction of God's fuller redemptive purpose. As our king he saves us from our sins (Matt 1:21), makes the new covenant in his own blood (26:26–29), which in turn lays the foundation for a new people of God (i.e., a new Israel), in the age to come he will manifest the kingdom of God in great power and overwhelming glory. In this sense, the new covenant follows the pattern of the Old, namely, the formation of a people, followed by the fulfillment of the promise of land, now conceived as a whole new creation (Rev 21:1–5).

Jesus' advent on the stage of world history some two thousand years ago is the connective tissue that links the successive Old Testament stages of fulfillment with God's new covenant and its successive stages of fulfillment. The expanding pattern can be condensed into its basic contours by focusing on the various segments of fulfillment along the lines of the above remarks: People (Israel)—Land (Canaan)—King (David and descendants)—King (the promised greater son of David)—People (Jews and Gentiles joined in Christ)—Land (a new, everlasting creation). In short, old and new covenant correspond to each other in mirror fashion with the promise of a people and land and the promise of a king forming the central link:

Old Covenant	*New Covenant*
People – Land – King	**King – People – Land**

So again, Jesus' coming was the key and decisive step to establish the kingdom of God. With the one king now seated on the

INTRODUCTION

eternal throne of the kingdom, all remaining pieces of the puzzle will fall into place. However, the coming of the kingdom took an unanticipated shape. Contrary to the people's eschatological horizon, the king of Israel was crucified, and his reign did not interfere with, let alone overthrow, Roman rule, at least not in any political or military sense. For the time being, the kingdom came in a way that no one had envisaged or foreseen.

This is the point where Jesus' parables fulfill their divine purpose. They teach old things (known from the Old Testament history of revelation) and new things (Matt 13:52), things that did not square with, or rather, exploded people's expectations. His kingdom stories were designed to deliver a vision of God's reign in the present time as an interim until the kingdom's grand unveiling in the consummation at the end of the age. The selection of stories in Matthew 13:1–52 intends to provide a summary view of the most salient aspects of God's rule in the era between the two advents of Christ, according to Jesus' own teachings. Along with the rest of the parables, it offers a window into Jesus' vision of the kingdom as we still experience it today. Some of its new aspects may not seem so new to us twenty-first-century readers, but it is the burden of this work to help appreciate the "newness" of the kingdom afresh. We can begin by reminding ourselves that the parables of the kingdom are indeed unique, insofar as they were meant to fulfill a very distinctive purpose at a critical junction in God's plan of redemption. They create a theological seam between the old and new covenants, old and new revelation. Moses taught the law to establish the theocratic kingdom of Israel. In essence, his instructions governed the religious life of Israel in Canaan with a Davidic king in Jerusalem. Jesus, on the other hand, as the greater son of David, established the kingdom of God that will last forever by telling stories. To these stories we shall now turn.

1

The Kingdom Requires a Decision

IN THE 2015 DRAMA *Mr. Holmes*, the now ninety-seven-year-old legendary detective attempts to solve the greatest mystery of his life: Why did he retire thirty-five years ago? The ensuing investigation into his past life is hampered by memory loss, but eventually, the truth begins to take shape, and the great Sherlock Holmes manages to put the pieces of the puzzle together for one last time. What he discovers is that he had refused to get personally involved with someone in a difficult case. The masterclass private investigator had always had the accolade of being a supremely rational person, whose famous ability to solve mysteries depended on focusing on facts and not emotions. Thus, he would never become entangled in any relationship. His stubborn refusal caused a death. The experience forced him to resign from his profession and haunted him for the rest of his life. In the end, Holmes has to come to terms with the truth that the missing solution, not only to the mystery but to his own happiness, is a simple decision: he must allow himself to get personally involved with people.

In the same way, everyone faces the decision to get personally involved with God. Jesus' teaching about the kingdom of God calls for the decision to take him at his word, the most crucial decision any human will make in his/her life. It is as dramatic as a man's

The Kingdom Requires a Decision

mishap, taking a tumble over a cliff, but grasping a branch on his way to the bottom a thousand feet below. His strength fading, he cries, "God, if you're real, save me, and I will trust and obey you with all my heart!" Then a mighty voice roars through the canyon: "So they all say when in trouble!" The man replies, "No, God, I mean it, I swear, save me!" "So be it," says the voice, "I will save you. Let go of that branch, and I will catch and carry you." "Let go of the branch? Am I crazy?" the man shrieks, and he wakes up—it was only a dream. But throwing yourself at God's feet is like freefall; it is all or nothing, with no plan B. It was so when people heard Jesus, whose teaching always forced a radical decision to embrace his new word of the kingdom.

The opening story of Matthew 13 is the parable of the sower (13:1–9, 18–23). The imagery of sowing, soils, and harvesting were certainly recognizable metaphors of the Old Testament. Jeremiah 31:27 identifies God as the sower, saying, "The days are coming, declares the LORD, when I will sow the house of Israel and the house of Judah with the seed of man and the seed of beast." The coming days are then specified as the era of a new covenant (31:31–34). Sowing seed, therefore, was no novel idea, but connected with Israel's eschatological expectations (see also Ezek 36:9 and Hos 2:23 for the same motif), as well as the annual agrarian life cycle of sowing, growing, and ingathering that so defined their existence. But in the parable of the sower, one must not miss the most obvious: The sower is the Son of Man (Matt 13:37)! Jesus does not merely act like an Old Testament prophet, declaring God's word, but he boldly asserts his right to share the privileges of God.[1] As Craig Blomberg notes with regard to Christ's prophetic predecessors, "Never did such individuals apply symbols for God to themselves so consistently as did Jesus, and none ever claimed that he was doing precisely what the Scriptures said God himself would do."[2] Here, in Jesus' self-identification with the sower, he claims to do what God had previously promised to perform. In doing so, he assumed cosmic stature and went well beyond what any

---

1. For a fine discussion, see Payne, "Jesus' Implicit Claim," 2–23.
2. Blomberg, *Interpreting the Parables*, 320.

prophet would have said about himself, which makes Jesus someone new or different, set apart from the line of God's spokesmen of the past. Jesus filling the role of the sower is Jesus putting on God's shoes, a veiled reference to his deity, or at the very least a reference to his unparalleled closeness to the Father. Seen in context, the first of the seven parables entails the bombshell of a sensational claim.

Surely, his contemporaries expected the kingdom of God to come with unmistakable signs of authenticity. Jesus' opponents never tired of asking for such signs,[3] although they had witnessed the miracles that he performed in their midst. But the parable of the sower at the beginning of this distinguished discourse sends out an important signal. Yes, Jesus performed signs of various kinds, and they confirmed the message of his preaching that the kingdom had finally arrived (cf. Mark 1:15). But primarily the kingdom "is not coming with signs to be observed" (Luke 17:20), but through a word that requires a *decision*. Only an unqualified positive response to the word of God's reign and to the person who calls himself the Son of Man will do to have a part in his kingdom. It cannot be had apart from him.

On the one hand, this is nothing new. From the very beginning, God's word called for a life-or-death decision. In the garden of Eden, God placed two trees at the heart of the primeval sanctuary, the tree of death (tree of knowing good and evil, Gen 2:16–17) and the tree of life. In conjunction with the prohibition to eat of the former upon penalty of death, the scenario confronted Adam and Eve with a basic decision, the choice between life and death.[4] At the conclusion of the covenant renewal in the plains of Moab, Moses summarized the whole Law in terms of a choice of life and death that echoed the language of the two trees in Eden. "See, I have set before you today life and good, death and evil . . . I call heaven and earth to witness against you today, that I have set

---

3. Matt 12:38; 16:1; Mark 8:11; Luke 11:16; John 2:18; 6:30. The request for a sign to validate Jesus' messianic identity is strongly reflected in all four Gospels. It was a common, recurring challenge.

4. For a more detailed discussion, see Emmrich, "The Temptation Narrative," 3–20.

The Kingdom Requires a Decision

before you life and death, blessing and curse. Therefore, choose life that you and your offspring may live" (Deut 30:15, 19). The prophet Jeremiah exhorted Zedekiah to submit to God's word in the context of the looming exile. But, as if possessed by an indomitable deathwish, the last king of Judah refused to listen. Jeremiah's response reflected the king's absurd suicidal decision: "Why will you and your people die by the sword, by famine, and by pestilence, as the LORD has spoken . . . ?" (Jer 27:13). In the same way, Ezekiel called on Israel: "Cast away from you all the transgressions that you have committed, and make yourselves a new heart and a new spirit! Why will you die, O house of Israel? For I have no pleasure in the death of anyone, declared the Lord GOD; so turn, and live" (Ezek 18:31–32, cf. 33:11).

God's word requires a positive response, for in hearing it, we encounter the authority of heaven itself (cf. Matt 21:23–36), and the history of God's dealings with his covenant people Israel confirms this. The word has always called for a decision. On the other hand, the parable of the sower hints at something novel in the way the word confronts us. During the times of the old covenant, the word came to an established people, bounded by national identity, the people of Israel. Their decision to hear and to do the word was a decision of life and death. But the covenantal setting in which this word occurred was assumed throughout the Old Testament. Here, in the parable of the sower, no such prerequisite is suggested. The word is *sown*, that is, scattered indiscriminately in some of the worst places imaginable! What farmer in his or her right mind would sow seed "along the path" (13:4), "on rocky ground" (13:5), or "among thorns" (13:7), rather than in the field that has been prepared and cultivated beforehand to receive it (13:8)?[5] Indeed, the surprising offense of the seemingly foolish sower who wastefully throws his precious seed all over the landscape is echoed

---

5. One might argue that the seed sown by the wayside, on rocky soil, or among thorns only fell there by accident. But if the seed sown on the good soil was sown there intentionally, then the same must apply to the rest of the "sowing." No distinction is indicated, but all that the sower does is purposeful.

by contrast at the very end of the discourse in the parable of the net.[6] The great dragnet is thrown into the sea and gathers aquatic creatures of every kind, both good and bad, before the catch is sorted out at the shore (13:47-48). With the images of indiscriminate scattering and gathering, respectively, the two parables form a delicate literary frame around the complex of seven stories in Matthew 13. The parable of the sower sets its sights on the beginning of the kingdom's coming, while the parable of the net portrays the end, and both have an inclusive or universal appeal with contrasting outward (sowing) and inward (gathering) locomotion. They therefore bring a pleasing sense of closure to the chapter as a whole.

The parable of the sower was already beginning to be fulfilled in Jesus' own teaching ministry. He addressed his word to everybody, with no distinction or discrimination. Tax collectors and harlots needed to hear it as well as the religious scribes and Pharisees.[7] Religious pedigree offered no advantage, nor did the lack of it pose a disadvantage with Jesus. His refusal to discriminate could even be expressed in words that shocked the religious leaders whose devotion was beyond dispute among the people: "Amen, I say to you, the tax collectors and the prostitutes go into the kingdom of God before you" (21:31). Jesus was not promoting affirmative action but repentance as the point of entry. Moreover, although his ministry was largely confined to Israel by his own definition (15:24), Jesus' final charge to the disciples made explicit that his word of good news was to go out to "all nations" (28:19), where the message would not meet with a people who were trained in a covenantal relationship with God (i.e., Israel), but where the word of God's reign would create new communities of faith by making disciples, people who responded to the challenge of the

---

6. Stanley D. Touissant notes the bookends by virtue of their placement and the absence of the introductory formula, "The kingdom of heaven is like..." in Touissant, "The Introductory and Concluding Parables," 351-55.

7. It stands to reason that notorious sinners did not frequent the temple or the synagogue, where religious Israelites used to congregate. They were outsiders, and yet, "the tax collectors and sinners were all drawing near to hear him" (Luke 15:1).

The Kingdom Requires a Decision

decision. It would succeed, for wherever the word is sown, it solicits a response, and, as the parable indicates, while many reject the word, some of the hearers receive it by "bearing fruit and yielding" (13:23). In this sense, the story of the sower implies a breach between Jesus the sower and his former people. Israel is no more the privileged people to whom God grants his revelation, but in the rejection of Jesus' message, the rift between God and Israel widens to the breaking point. The sower numbers the days of national Israel as God's covenant people. What establishes the Israel and kingdom of God from now on is a proper response to the seed of the word without ethnic or any other distinctions. Jesus' parable flew in the face of his people's expectations, who, in their reading of the Old Testament, never saw God's kingdom coming so quietly and hidden merely through the proclamation of a word.[8]

According to the story, an unqualified positive response to the word of the kingdom implies two elemental aspects: "hearing and understanding" (13:19, 23), and perseverance (13:20–23). The kingdom of God calls for a decision, but also for a constant reaffirmation of the choice, which translates into endurance. We must continue to live in the choice that we once made if the word is to bear any fruit in our lives. It will need to be reaffirmed in faith and repentance.

"Hearing and understanding" provide a conspicuous frame for Jesus' commentary on the parable. Those along the path (13:19) lack what the good soil has (13:23), namely hearing and understanding, or, rather, hearing *with* understanding. Hearing without understanding results in total loss: both the seed and the hearer are lost. Jesus' appeal to hearing and understanding does not mean that his parables were or are too difficult to comprehend. Intellectual acumen won't keep people out of the kingdom. After all, it belongs to children, too (19:14). But what Jesus has in mind is signaled by his reference to "the evil one" (13:19), snatching away the word like ravenous birds. Hearing and understanding are part of a spiritual—not physical or intellectual—reality. The act of hearing may be no more than a reflex, hearing words that are spoken

8. Ladd, *The Presence of the Future*, 225.

audibly. All four types in the story share the ability to hear. Yet, hearing with understanding means more than just making sense of the message received. I can say, "Jesus died for me," and claim to understand the meaning of the sentence. Whether or not I also believe the words and make them my own, however, is quite a different matter. "Understanding" here means, "This is for me, my entire existence depends on this word!" It is time that we appreciate the supernatural marvel that lies over our lives when we hear the word of the kingdom and realize that God really means *me*. We need a certain new ingenuousness or naiveté that knows that we are children of God and wants to remain so. In this sense, hearing is what most people don't see, the reason, the ultimate reason to commit to the word of the kingdom.

In 1 Corinthians 1:23, the apostle Paul sketches the rejection of the gospel in terms of two basic agendas: "For Jews demand signs and Greeks seek wisdom, but we preach Christ crucified, a stumbling block to Jews and folly to Gentiles" To those who are religiously inclined (represented by "Jews"), the cross of Christ may seem odious, for how could God have his Son nailed to a tree? Or, if his death was indeed for us, are we really as bad as to call for such desperate measures? Yet again, to those who seek wisdom (represented by the "Greeks") and rely on man's reason to construct reality, the idea of God come in the flesh to die on a cross is either a fairy tale or a fool's tale. How can enlightened individuals of the twenty-first century still believe in a myth?

Whatever form the rejection of the word may take, it is also part of a spiritual reality that keeps people in unbelief. As Jesus indicates in the parable, there is an evil one who is in the business of snatching away the truth as soon as it is heard. 2 Corinthians 4:3–4 describes the process in the following way: "And even if our gospel is veiled, it is veiled only to those who are perishing. In their case the god of this world has blinded the minds of the unbelievers, to keep them from seeing the light of the gospel of the glory of Christ, who is the image of God." We might say that God is at a certain disadvantage (though he never is) because the glory of Christ is not easily discerned from the perspective of his crucifixion. For

The Kingdom Requires a Decision

whatever could be seen in or said about him is canceled or relativized by the cross. To make the word of the cross palatable to an unbeliever requires more than just skillful rhetoric, good will, or determination. The gospel is good news only to those who also hear its bad news. Hearing with understanding implies receiving the word as one's only hope, answering our absolute need of God's forgiveness in Jesus Christ. This is the decision that is required by the word of God's reign.

But even if the gospel carries this claim, the world has its own way of accounting for the way things are. "Why, I am not going to hang my whole life on a word like this! There have been many religious fanatics, and where are they now? Besides, we know that God or the old man upstairs is nothing but wishful thinking. Only people who aren't cut out for this life believe in a crucified Savior—schmucks!" In this way and a thousand more, the evil one snatches away the word that is sown in the heart. It is by default a thought process determined by the value system cultivated in a given society and accepted by the individual. Yet the spiritual blinding is as much a reality as Tolkien suggested in Sauron's sinister scheme engraved on the One Ring: "One ring to rule them all, one ring to find them, one ring to bring them all, and in the darkness bind them."

Hearing with understanding can occur with considerable delay, just as seed sown may take a long time to germinate. In his biography of the eighteenth-century preacher John Newton, Aitken writes of a dream that Newton had during his years at sea.[9] In this dream, Newton received a ring from a mysterious supernatural figure. The ring carried the promise of keeping Newton happy and safe. But a second supernatural being persuaded him to throw the ring into the sea. As soon as the ring vanished in the dark, Newton himself sank into a nightmare of despair and distress. Then a third being appeared who went after the ring and recovered it from the deep. Newton asked him whether he could have it back, but the stranger informed him that he would retain the ring for safekeeping until such a time when it could be returned to him. Newton

---

9. Aitken, *John Newton*, 37–38.

was convinced that this dream spoke about his childhood faith, abandoned like the ring, waiting to be found again and returned at a later point in his life.

Whether or not hearing with understanding comes with delay or not, the kingdom of God calls for a decision on the part of the hearer, and hearing with understanding is the prerequisite. The choice, in essence, is of the same fabric as Israel's choice of life and death under the old covenant, but it comes in the context of a far more liberal application of the word. No longer "sown" into a covenantal community, it is now scattered all across the earth in uncultivated places where no sower would sow his seed. The parable therefore intimates that Jesus had a clear vision of the universal appeal of his gospel that would ring out to the ends of the earth (Acts 1:8). As Paul said in Athens, "The times of ignorance God overlooked, but now he commands all people everywhere to repent, because he has fixed a day on which he will judge the world in righteousness by a man whom he has appointed; and of this he has given assurance to all by raising him from the dead" (Acts 17:30–31). This appeal contains the bookends of the parable of the sower and of the net, the call to return to God and the final judgment at the end of the age. A decision must be made for or against God's kingdom.

But, as is also clear from the parable, the decision can never be divorced from the present day. Unless it is reaffirmed and applied in ever-new ways, the kingdom will soon be lost (or has never been in one's possession), as when a boat is taken out into the open sea by a steady current with little or no friction, and before long land is out of sight. The train that seemed bound for its destination is derailed. The seed sown among rocks and thorns tells the tale of failure to persevere in the faith. The two scenarios are very similar, both stressing the need for endurance, but each makes its own contribution.

The rocky soil, where the seed germinates quickly but is soon scorched by the blazing sun (Matt 13:6), is rendered in 13:20–21 in the following way: "As for what was sown on rocky ground, this is the one who hears the word and immediately receives it with

The Kingdom Requires a Decision

joy, yet he has no root in himself, but endures for a while, and when tribulation and persecution arises on account of the word, immediately he falls away." As Leon Morris puts it, "Plants with defective root systems are not equipped to handle the hot weather."[10] Twice the word "immediately" is used here. Easy come, easy go, one could say. This type of person rises like a comet and disappears forever like a burned-out star. Endurance lasts for a while, but when put to the test by hardship on account of the gospel, the person is shown for what he is. I wonder whether John Bunyan thought of this parable when he introduced the character Pliable, who joyfully commits to the pilgrimage to the celestial city but bails out at the first sign of trouble.[11]

No one should be surprised by persecution. Jesus himself was crucified, and since then, countless followers have suffered for their faith. After all, "it has been granted to you for the sake of Christ that you should not only believe in him but also suffer for his sake" (Phil 1:29). Hardship on account of following Christ was something well-known to the apostle Paul, who also said, "all who desire to live a godly life in Christ Jesus will be persecuted" (2 Tim 3:12). More will be said about this in our discussion of the parable of the weeds. But there is another, more subtle attack on the kingdom of God in this world. It comes into view in "what was sown among thorns" (Matt 13:22). Since the cross, the enemy has used intimidation in some places, but he also comes through deception, scheming, and allurements in other places, a means just as dangerous and effective. The situation can be illustrated in terms of two detectives conducting an interrogation. The first waves his fist in the suspect's face, grabbing him by the neck, and threatens to beat the truth out of him. The second is a very different character, gentle, respectful, and thoughtful. He even intervenes on behalf of the suspect, turning to him to ask, "What can I get you? A cup of coffee, yes? Sugar, cream? All right!" He returns with the cup in hand and says, "Now, you understand, I'm here to help you. But I can't help you unless you give me something . . ." We know

---

10. Morris, *The Gospel According to Matthew*, 337.
11. Bunyan, *Pilgrim's Progress*, 27–32.

the good-cop-bad-cop theme from popular films. But despite the contrast of characters, they are after the same thing. So it is with the rocky soil and the thorns. The former pictures persecution as a frontal assault on the professor's faith. The thorns, on the other hand, are like the gentle cop, who gets what he wants by way of diplomacy and fake concern.

Thus, Jesus speaks of the care of this world and the deceitfulness of riches choking the word of the kingdom like thorns (13:22). The loss in this case in no less total than in the first two scenarios. This warning is as relevant today as it ever has been. "The care of this world" is everything that we consider important in our postmodern culture. The media bring its spirit into nearly every home 24/7. It is inculcated at our universities in English 101 and has been so since the 1960s. There is no absolute truth, but a new tolerance that says, "You must not fail to affirm my views, and you must have no deep convictions that call into question the validity of other people's views! If what you believe works for you, that's okay, I'm glad for you, but don't you impose the conviction of your own interpretive community on us!" Moral relativism and the new tolerance have eroded the call of the gospel to repent of sin. Therefore, Christians can easily be handed off as obscurantists, bigots, misanthropes, and haters of all people. They dare not obstruct the path of diversity, change, choice, and tolerance.[12]

Herbert Schlossberg[13] attacks modern idols, such as humanism, consumerism, naturalism, power, and entertainment, which inhabit our knowledge industry, powered by technologically enhanced communication like a global megaphone. Lies in the form of ideas (for example, that we are basically all good people, but some of us have been victimized) float freely through the air. Opinions and values that used to take decades or longer to take root in a society are now shaped virtually overnight and reach all people everywhere via the information superhighway. Idolatrous ideas are pervasive and all the more insidious because they are

---

12. A good discussion of this is found in Stetson and Conti, *The Truth about Tolerance*, 86–97.

13. Schlossberg, *Idols*.

atmospheric. Our cultural value judgments and worldview tend to be assumed rather than argued. We are brainwashed to think that it's all so obvious, that anyone who is with it knows how things are. People are no more aware of the current of ideas in which they are floating downstream than the fish is aware of the water in which it swims! We are taken by and drown in the cultural stream.

The miracles of modern science and technology are also doing their part in moving Christians away from simple faith in the Christ of the gospel to invest their hope in progress and limitless possibilities. Technology and progress are not evil in and of themselves, but they have become idols. The common sentiment is, "How could we possibly be wrong, when endless possibilities lie in front of us? Progress in science shows the superiority of our ideas and way of life over those of the past." In this way, technology makes us believe that there is surpassing power residing in the human spirit and in our most refined worldview. We worship at the shrine of technology and at the feet of the experts. The reign of experts and informed insiders has become particularly obvious during the recent COVID-19 crisis, as the pronouncements of virologists have been telling us what to think and how to respond, even if many of them contradicted each other.

Our idolatrous culture, with its concerns, angst, and riches, is a powerful tool of the enemy, now more than ever, because of the proliferation of information. In our world, political or religious institutions don't kill people. They don't have to. But the pressure to conform to cultural conventions and values is enormous. COVID-19 has finally revealed the oppressive nature of public sentiment, as anyone who disagrees can readily be branded as unloving or reckless with regards to common welfare and the love of neighbor. If you don't play by the rules of the system (or the crisis as it is portrayed), you will be declared socially unfit and marginalized. Misfits, on the other hand, are all the more the targets of social engineering, reeducation, and reprogramming according to the norms of culture to become good citizens of the brave new world. George Orwell is beckoning. To this end, we use education, financial penalties and various inducements, and the relentless onslaught of the media to form our values and decisions. Meanwhile, unnoticed by the world, the whole megasystem functions in a mysterious way to make people stay clear of facing the one decision placed in front of us in the gospel. Moreover, to further obscure our most pressing need, we are inundated with a flood of choices because choice is sold as an inviolable good. In previous generations, making decisions was not felt as pressure, as far fewer choices were available. But now, nearly everything, including marriage, sexual orientation, career, and lifestyle, are up for the taking. Life has become a maelstrom of confusing decisions; as Martin Seligman notes, "The modern individual is not the peasant of yore with a fixed future yawning ahead. He—and now she, effectively doubling the market—is a battleground of decisions and preferences."[14] We don't face the sword, but untangling ourselves from the thorns of cultural idols and a maze of choices and decisions is nearly impossible. The word of the kingdom is choked, and when it is, the evangelical Christian is hardly distinguishable from anyone else and the church becomes a country club. As Jesus says, "it (the word) proves unfruitful" (13:22).

Of the first three soils, the third typifies professing Christians who, unlike the previous two, may stick around and maintain at least an outward appearance of Christian life in the communities of faith, but their unfruitfulness may indicate that they have failed to persevere all the same. They still wear the team's jersey, but are sitting on the bench. The decision that they once made upon hearing the word has not been confirmed in their lives. The desires for worldly security, prosperity, affirmation (or fear of shame), beauty, the so-called "good life," and the American dream have replaced and so choked the word of the kingdom. Indeed, the grip of worldly values is not only holding sway over university campuses, corporate America, shopping malls, and the media. The norms of culture are also inside our churches. We are seduced to make peace with the world and to conform to common values. So, when political powers ordered the shutdown of church worship in person due to the threat of coronavirus, Christians more or less

---

14. Quoted in Buie, "'Me' Decades," 18.

The Kingdom Requires a Decision

unanimously submitted in the name of public safety, safety being one of our idols. Gathering in person, so it appears, has to be safe, and when it is not, the evangelical Christian withholds worship of the God of glory. Since God never gave us a guarantee to keep worship risk-free in any scenario, the re-shifting of Christian priorities has been revealed. The health-and-wealth theology in the mold of Joel Osteen, propagating the mantra of prosperity and pop psychology, has long and rightly been criticized as a betrayal of the cross, but the overriding concern for personal health appears to be more insidious among Christians even of the more conservative wing. Appearances can be deceiving.

But the word does not fail. There is a positive response. "As for what was sown on good soil, this is the one who hears the word and understands it. He indeed bears fruit and yields, in one case a hundredfold, in another sixty, and in another thirty" (13:23).[15] As the present aspect of "bearing" (ποιεῖ) fruit indicates, the good *keeps on* producing. The decision to live under God's reign is affirmed by a habit of good works irrespective of the circumstances, that is, despite the enemy's attempted "snatching" (soil 1), despite persecution (soil 2), and despite the world's temptations (soil 3). In some way, what proves to be detrimental to the other three types cannot keep the "good" type from bearing fruit. It does so and perseveres in it, rain or shine.

Critical in this conflict is that we continue to have our thinking informed and shaped by biblical truth (Rom 12:1–2), not secular values. Jesus' parable describes the organic process in a trajectory of *hearing—understanding (faith)—fruit (doing)*. Fruit-bearing naturally follows the preceding two things. But the process always involves conflict and struggle. No Christian in Christ's church should ever wonder whether spiritual warfare is on or not. We can safely assume that we are in the midst of it. Church leadership and every member of Christ's local body must remain alert to the constant reality of the tug-of-war over our souls in order to bear fruit and to renew and confirm our decision daily in countless

---

15. Jesus' reference here is no hyperbole or exaggeration. The yield is true-to-life in an agrarian setting.

applications. A fine Christian prayer is, "Father, I love you. I trust you. I am yours, and as long as you are present in my life, I really don't need anything to make me happy." Here is fruit!

Overall, the parable of the sower suggests that we can expect rejection of the kingdom message along with fruit. Since Jesus' day, when the coming of the kingdom was first proclaimed and took many by surprise, resulting in much rejection, nothing in essence has changed. There will be losing and winning, but we can join the work of the Son of Man in sowing the seed with confidence wherever we go. If we have heard the word of the kingdom, it is our responsibility to understand the word, our mission to plant the word like seed, and to expect a whole range of responses to it.

2

The Kingdom as God's Decision

THE HUMAN BEING IS a curious specimen. He always wants to know the reason for things. As soon as you have one of us, you will hear the question "Why?" Children tirelessly raise the query to their parents, and we never stop asking it. We are wired to investigate, interpret data or words, and to get to the bottom of a matter. The parable of the sower brings up an important question: What accounts for the contrast between the first three types of soils that represent total loss and the fecund, high-yielding good soil? Are some people better than others? Do some have a leg up on others? Who or what makes the difference? Matthew 13:10–17, the first of three interpretive commentaries built into the collection of parables, furnishes a theological answer. Yes, the kingdom always requires a decision on the part of the hearer of its message, but the kingdom is also a decision that has already been made by God on behalf of those who are destined to obtain the gift of hearing. Hearing and believing (understanding), as the sower speaks of them, are a gift from God that is not granted indiscriminately. God reserves it for his elect people. It is something like a "529 Plan." A 529 plan is a college savings plan with tax benefits. Every year, Americans invest millions of dollars in such accounts to offset the astronomical costs of college education. When their children come of age, the accrued savings will be available to pay for hair-raising tuitions and other related expenses. Sometimes parents enroll their children in a 529 plan even before they are born. In a similar way, God has made a decision to bless his elect children with the knowledge of the mysteries of the kingdom in his own time, when his children come of age. For Jesus' disciples, the time had finally come, for they were to be schooled and participate in the inbreaking rule of God.

The disciples want to know why Jesus so courted the habit of speaking in parables (13:10). So, here is another one of those "Why" questions, and Jesus' reply is telling: "To you it has been given to know the secrets of the kingdom of heaven, but to them it has not been given" (13:11). "To be given" is a divine passive, God being the giver of this knowledge of the kingdom. Jesus uses an important qualifier. It is the "secrets" (mysteries, μυστήρια) of the kingdom that God reveals to his people via Jesus' parables. The term is the first clear signal of something new, something that the Old Testament prophets had not known or seen, namely that the much-anticipated coming of God's reign is hidden, as if working quietly behind the scenes. The Jewish expectation involved a divine intervention that would rival, if not surpass, the exodus from Egypt with a tangible political and geographical revolution for the people of Israel, not some mystery, or a covert operation. Jewish hopes rested on a king of David's lineage to come and restore the kingdom to Israel as a sovereign state.[1]

The advent of David's son would spell the end of foreign (Roman) occupation and usher in a golden age of *shalom* and unprecedented prosperity, not unlike the Christian teaching of premillennialism. But Jesus' words suggest that the manifestation of God's rule is not accessible to every Israelite, and the ambiguity indicated by the term "secrets" was not part of the eschatological horizon of Jesus' Jewish contemporaries. No one saw the restoration coming in two distinct stages, but this is the mystery that Jesus now revealed in their hearing. As he later taught them, the mystery

---

1. The expectation was evidently shared by Jesus' own disciples, as is clear from Acts 1:6.

The Kingdom as God's Decision

was already contained in the Old Testament Scriptures (cf. Luke 24:44), but only to such a degree that it can now be seen in the light of his coming. Prior to Christ, God's plan for the kingdom was like a sealed book, waiting to be opened in "the last days" (Dan 12:9).

The last days and the time of restoration promised throughout the Old Testament began with the coming of Jesus the Messiah. As he himself affirmed upon his resurrection, "All authority in heaven and on earth" are now his, and the mystery has been unveiled. Nonetheless, in a certain sense, the mystery remains, because his reign is still hidden and contested by many until his return on the last day of the last days. Only then will the Son of Man "gather out of his kingdom all causes of sin and all law-breakers" (Matt 13:41; cf. 1 Cor 15:25). So, in this interim period, the kingdom of God does not come with unmistakable attestation that forces everyone to their knees. It certainly was not so in Jesus' own ministry, or else his people would not have crucified him. The reign of Christ is apparent only to those who (paradoxically) fix their eyes on things not apparent or in plain sight, and they do this only because it has been given to them to know and to see. While real and present, the kingdom still must be revealed to be discerned (cf. John 3:3). John writes, "By this we know love, that he laid down his life for us" (1 John 3:16), but not everyone can or is willing to see this. God must translate or *interpret* the message of the kingdom for the individual to truly bring it home to the heart. Seeing the kingdom is seeing Jesus. Knowing it is knowing him, a personal revelation that is the key to seeing God's truth about the kingdom (cf. Gal 1:16).

A father thought that he could steal some time from his son by cutting a magazine photo of planet Earth into dozens of pieces, saying, "Here, son, why don't you work on putting this little puzzle together for me? And when you're done, Daddy will play with you!" But to his consternation, the boy returned within minutes with the finished job. "How did you do it? The picture has so many details," Daddy wanted to know. The son answered, "Oh, that was easy! The flipside was the picture of a man. I put him together, piece of cake, and then I turned the puzzle over, and there was the earth." In the same way, God makes us see the Son as the key to his plan for the world that is not apparent to the naked eye.

In this respect, Jesus' habit of teaching in parables is a perfect match for the veiled coming of the kingdom. A parable requires an act of translation, as the surface meaning of the story *per se* has little or nothing to do with God's reign.[2] The situation is not unlike the illustration of the father's makeshift puzzle, where the son not only knows that the finished product shows planet Earth, but goes to work on putting together the person that is shown on the reverse side of the page. In the case of a parable, it is not that the act of translation is too difficult or can be accomplished only by a select few experts in hermeneutics. The story itself functions as a sign of the nature of the kingdom's mode of event in the present time. It is already here, but hidden under (or within) the apparent words that form the story. So the kingdom is a free gift to those to whom it has been given (revealed), a gift that is withheld from others who do not believe.

As for those who reject the message, Jesus clinches the point in Matthew 13:13: "This is why I speak to them in parables, because seeing they do not see, and hearing they do not hear, nor do they understand." The parables are thus also a sign to the unbelievers. They can very well see the images of which the stories speak (i.e., they can develop a mental image of seed, field, treasure, etc.), just as they can hear the words that come from Jesus' lips, but they do not take it to heart and the translation of the word of the kingdom to the heart fails. The hidden message gets lost in translation. One may even grasp the import of the images in how they convey the nature of the kingdom, but unless the parable is received and embraced as absolute truth and ultimate reality, real understanding is withheld. As Isaiah 6:9–10 says, "This people's heart has grown dull." Isaiah and all the prophets characterized

---

2. Of course, every speech act requires translation on account of the semiotic nature of human words and language as a whole. Yet a parable in its very nature involves speaking of one reality in terms of another, parallel reality and thus necessitates the act of translating the surface meaning of the story into the deeper reality or hidden meaning conveyed through the parable's apparent images and plot.

The Kingdom as God's Decision

Israel's obtuse condition of not heeding God's word as their own choice, but this is only what appears to the naked eye. The dullness of the people is also a sovereign act of God's judgment,[3] confirming them in the decision that they have made to reject the prophetic message[4] and withholding healing from God that comes through repentance (13:15).

At this point, we can also appreciate the placement of the parable of the sower and its interpretive commentary. Both provide a theological perspective of the hostility against Jesus and his word that reaches a first climax in Matthew 12. The parable and its interpretation explain the underlying spiritual reason why the message of the kingdom is resisted rather than received.[5] On the one hand, the rejection of Jesus' teaching is nothing new. It is the continuing tale of the people of Israel whom the prophets characterized as blind and deaf (Isa 42:18–19). But there is a sense in which the situation is now even more acute. Jesus hints at this truth when he says, "Indeed, in their case the prophecy of Isaiah is fulfilled" (Matt 13:14). The culpability of the people as well as God's hardening of their hearts are heightened in the climactic ministry of Jesus because the kingdom has now come. Israel's judgment therefore also moves to its final phase as part of the kingdom's final and definitive unveiling in Jesus. This is the fullness of time (Mark 1:15), the promised restoration, and the blindness and deafness of Jesus' contemporaries will reach its ultimate expression in the crucifixion of the King himself. Here is the ultimate revelation of the kingdom, and here is the ultimate and full meaning of Isaiah's pronouncement of judgment. Jesus speaking in parables is a sign of this judgment taking a turn for the worse. On one hand, his stories convey their true significance by a divine act of translation, but the flipside is that they are also God's tool of judgment ringing in the final phase of the old curse of Israel's obtuseness.

---

3. The act of judgment must also be viewed as an aspect of God's in-breaking reign, as Jesus explained to Nicodemus in John 3:16–21.

4. Isa 6:10 is explicit, as God commands his prophet, "*Make* the heart of this people fat, and their eyes heavy, and blind their eyes . . ."

5. Cf. Bailey, "The Parable of the Sower and the Soils," 178.

If the prophets preached judgment in the form of a hardening of hearts, Jesus' parable of the sower, the parable of all parables, now certifies that no national covenantal privileges will secure Israel's salvation apart from taking his word to heart by true repentance. Many refused the message of the parables because God hardened their hearts precisely beyond repentance.

Only a proper response to his word will open the gates to the kingdom to those who believe. As Jesus said in his parable of the tenants, "The kingdom of God will be taken away from you and given to a people producing its fruit. And the one who falls on this stone will be broken to pieces; and when it falls on anyone, it will crush him" (Matt 21:43-44). The kingdom is "given" and at the same time "not given" as an act of judgment. So the parables of Jesus portend the final stage of God's judgment on his recalcitrant people. "Not all who are descended from Israel belong to Israel, and not all are children of Abraham because they are his offspring" (Rom 9:6-7).

Both the translation of the message as well as Israel's judgment rest on God's initiative. He has to grant the knowledge of the mysteries of the kingdom, and this is why Jesus calls this gift a "blessing" in Matthew 13:16-17 as he resumes his discourse on the secrets of his reign that are revealed to his chosen. "But blessed are your eyes, for they see, and your ears, for they hear. For truly, I say to you, many prophets and righteous people have longed to see what you see, and did not see it, and to hear what you hear, and did not hear it." Jesus' beatitude affirms that the time of his ministry is a new thing in the sense of 13:52 ("what is new"), God's fulfillment of the promise of redemption that was shared by "many prophets and righteous people" without ever witnessing its realization. But it is also new in that the blinding of Israel finally reaches its summit. Isaiah asked about the duration of the blinding, "How long, O LORD?" God's answer was, "Until cities lie waste without inhabitant" (6:11). Only now does the image of waste cities without inhabitants become clear. It is a spiritual wasteland, due to Israel's unbelief, and it reached its ultimate height in the rejection of Jesus

The Kingdom as God's Decision

and his word at the end of a long line of prophetic precursors who met the same fate. Hans Conzelmann's idea of the "center of time" comes to mind,[6] a brief, unprecedented, and unrepeatable period of absolutely unique quality in God's redemptive program. The time has now come in the ministry of Jesus, but there is a twist in the tale: to recognize the time is not up to the individual nor rests on personal acumen. Rather, it takes nothing less than God's blessing to see and to hear with understanding. The coming of the kingdom, despite the many extraordinary authenticating signs that Jesus performed, was *still* not self-evident to his people, nor did many make a decision to live and act in the reality of its advent, let alone confirmed such a decision from day to day.[7] They failed to see what God placed in front of them, not the least because God's attestation of Jesus as the Sent One culminated in his crucifixion, which did not square with the people's notion of the promised deliverer. Nevertheless, the secrets of the kingdom through Jesus *were* given to those whom the Father had chosen to bless, making the *givenness* of the kingdom a mystery or secret of its own. Many hear the same story, but only some embrace the narrative as their own, the lens of ultimate reality through which everything else is seen, interpreted, and understood.

The absolute, personal surrender to the sown word is above all the result of the decision that none less than God himself has made for his people and against his recalcitrant people of Israel, notwithstanding a faithful remnant. God grants the knowledge of the kingdom's secrets to some and along with it makes known his hidden counsel (cf. Ps 25:4). He makes his appeal to all people, but he reveals the secrets of his reign only to some. The parable of the sower is timelessly denotative of this process, just as Jesus was conscious of the dynamics of this divine gift, granted to his disciples for the time being, while many were hardened and remained

---

6. Conzelmann, *Die Mitte der Zeit*.

7. As the Gospels relate, in Jesus' final entry of Jerusalem (Matt 21:1–11; Luke 19:28–40), there were fleeting moments of commitment and euphoria, but no real faith on the greater part of Israel.

in darkness. He knew that God's story of redemption had moved to its final chapter in his coming, the beginning of the last days, and that God's judgment of Israel as a blind and deaf people had moved on to its final installment. Jesus was present, the king had arrived, but "he came to his own, and his own people did not receive him" (John 1:11). His final rejection would take shape in the crucifixion of the King and resulted in the subsequent carnage of the Jewish-Roman War of AD 66–70. Yet all of this was part of the master plan of the revelation of God's reign in Christ.

To summarize our findings in this chapter, we can highlight three distinct points. First, Jesus' use of the term "secrets" (mysteries) in conjunction with the parable of the sower indicates that the kingdom of God is revealed, but also remains veiled, contrary to popular expectations. The hiddenness of God's reign took everyone by surprise. Second, his commentary on the sower makes explicit that Israel will be redefined. There will be no more nationalistic privileges for the Old Testament people of God, but Israel is wherever the word of the kingdom is heard and understood with the result of bearing genuine fruit.[8] Jesus' words show his parables of kingdom secrets to be signs of divine judgment on Israel, a judgment that had now entered a new and final stage with profound implications for the present age. Third, knowing the secrets of the kingdom is a gift and therefore the blessing of God to the true Israel. Jesus speaks of knowing the secrets, but in a real sense, the givenness of the kingdom (knowing as a gift from God) is itself the mystery of God's inaugurated rule.[9] The kingdom of God is a decision that God already made for his elect people who have been (and will be) given ears to hear.[10]

---

8. This notion is emphatically confirmed in Acts. Time and again, the apostle Paul began his preaching in the context of the Jewish synagogue, but upon their rejection of the message of Jesus he turned to the Gentiles (Acts 13:46, 51; 18:6).

9. Jesus made this clear in emphatic fashion in his words to Peter in Matt 16:17 with the same beatific vocabulary that is found in 13:16–17 (i.e., "blessed").

10. Significantly, the parable of the sower closes with the telltale imperative: "He who has ears to hear, let him hear!" God himself will fulfill the

The Kingdom as God's Decision

Two thousand years after the events, many professing Christians who frequent today's churches are still as blind and deaf as ancient Israel. There is much talk of making a decision for Jesus, praying formulaic prayers, and feeling emotional responses to God's word. None of them are wrong in themselves, but they often indicate that our God is a domesticated version of the real person with whom we have to do. Yes, God always calls us to decide for him, but he also makes a decision for us. This mystery of the kingdom is as hard to fathom and accept as it was in Jesus' day. But all who come to him in true faith will eventually know that our seeking of him was due to his choice of seeking us. All we know and believe has its origin in his blessing of revealing to us the mysteries of his kingdom. He gave in the first place, and we receive. A 7-Eleven cashier raises his arms at two o'clock in the morning when he stares down the sawed-off barrel of a shotgun, an unmistakable sign of surrender, saying, "You can have anything you want." But we lift our hands in surrender and worship to God through Jesus Christ, and this surrender is our greatest victory. For unlike the cashier's reaction, it is not forced, but the result of God's blessing.

The French mathematician and philosopher Blaise Pascal (1623–62) never lived without pain after his eighteenth birthday. During the last decade of his life, he suffered from almost constant exhaustion and frequent swooning, which made his work exceedingly difficult. Yes, in his prayer "To Ask God for the Proper Use of Sickness," his surrender to God's greatness is on full display. He writes, "Thou alone knowest what is most expedient for me. Thou art the sovereign master, do what thou wilt. Give to me, take from me; but conform my will to thine."[11] In essence, Pascal prayed for God to continue to decide for him, as he had in the past. This also brings us to the next parable in Matthew 13, the parable of the weeds.

---

requirement of hearing ears, while at the same time, it is an encouragement to listeners to pay all the closer attention.

11. Lems, "On the Proper Use of Sickness (Pascal)."

3

The Kingdom Admits of Opposition

THE PARABLE OF THE sower suggests that, for the time being, the kingdom has been inaugurated, but not consummated. For the first-century Jewish audience, this would have been nothing short of shocking. The parable of the weeds and its commentary (Matt 13:24–30, 36–43) goes even further. Not only remains the kingdom a work in progress, but it is manifest in a world of sin and lawlessness (13:41).[1] The lines are drawn sharply. Whereas the parable

---

1. This is to some extent already implied in the parable of the sower's first three soils. Equating the kingdom with the premillennial view of Christ's earthly reign from Jerusalem (i.e., the millennial reign), a number of commentators view the parable of the weeds with its clear vision of open opposition not as a presentation of God's reign *per se* but only as a picture of what will eventually usher into the millennial kingdom. Mike Stallard, for example, argues that "The parable of the tares suggests that Jesus, in light of the rejection of him by the leaders of the nation of Israel, is teaching that the kingdom will not happen immediately. Instead, there will be a time of sowing in preparation for the future kingdom" (Stallard, "Hermeneutics and Matthew 13," 351). But the language of both the sower and the weeds militates against a time of mere preparation, short of a (partial but true) realization of the kingdom. "Hearing the word of the kingdom" (13:19) and "bearing fruit" (13:23) clearly suggest "the already" of the kingdom, as Jesus also hinted at in his words to Jewish antagonists: "The kingdom of God will be taken away from you and given to a people producing its fruits" (21:43). The "givenness" of the kingdom in turn correlates with the knowledge of "secrets of the kingdom of heaven" granted

The Kingdom Admits of Opposition

of the sower features four types (soils) of people, here the story reduces the cast of characters to only two kinds: the "good seed" (13:24) and the "weeds" (13:25). So the image of sowing remains a common property among the first two parables of the complex, but the weeds removes the complexities of the sower against the backdrop of a sweeping global panorama. With this simplification, the stage of the parable is now explicitly said to be the whole "world" (13:38) with two groups of people at opposite ends.[2]

But the parable also adds another salient point. There are now two "sowers," namely the "Son of Man" (13:37) and "the devil" (13:39).[3] Accordingly, the wheat and the weeds are the "sons of the kingdom" and the "sons of the evil one." The mention of an enemy itself is hardly novel. After all, the previous parable had already spoken of "the evil one" (13:19) as the snatcher of the seed. But while 13:19 casts his role in terms of snatching away the seed of the word, here his efforts are more overtly aggressive. Rather than taking something away, he deliberately sows his weeds into the field to compromise and ultimately destroy the good seed. Darnel (ζιζάνια, *zizania*, 13:25) is a plant unique to the Middle East. Botanically related to wheat, it is a fungal rye grass that grows within the wheat, yet is almost indistinguishable from the "good seed." Because wheat and weed grow with an intertwined root system, the latter cannot be removed without causing damage to the former.[4] But as the story makes clear, the master of the estate is not ignorant of the enemy's schemes (13:28). He allows it for the time being. The conclusion is inevitable: the kingdom of heaven

---

to those who have ears to hear (13:11). Then again, Jesus' portrait of judgment day as a "gathering out of his kingdom all causes of sin and all law-breakers" (13:41) most naturally requires the actual existence of the kingdom prior to the gathering out or the separation.

2. The Greek term for weeds is *zizania*. It refers to darnel, a rye grass that in its early growth resembles wheat. Wheat and weeds growing together in the field poses a dilemma to the farmer, because any attempt to uproot the weeds would also damage the roots of the wheat.

3. 13:28 leaves him unidentified as "a certain enemy," but 13:39 lifts the veil by calling him by name.

4. Zohary, *Plants of the Bible*, 161.

admits of opposition. Not only is conflict built into the scenario portrayed by the mixing of seeds in the field, but the kingdom will be sabotaged and suffer violence at the hands of the enemy and his henchfolks.

The conflict will continue until the end of the present age (13:41), which will thus be characterized by perplexing struggle and tension that did not belong to the eschatological horizon of Jesus' contemporaries. The interim period of conflict and suffering must come first, and only after this age will "the righteous shine like the sun in the kingdom of their Father" (13:43). The language of solar luminosity is an unmistakable allusion to Daniel 12:3, one of the few Old Testament texts that predict the resurrection at the end of time.[5] So, once again, the parable confirms the ambiguity that inheres the present manifestation of the kingdom already in the world, and in this sense would have disappointed the expectations of many who had hoped to see the kingdom come at once with overwhelming power, eliminating any opposition.

The sabotage of God's reign in the last days began with the rejection of King Jesus himself. Since his days, the church has suffered persecution, and there is no end in sight because the devil "has come down . . . in great wrath" (Rev 12:12). He wages war against the Son of Man and his people in the world with relentless fury. The World Watch List, published annually by the organization Open Doors, monitors Christian persecution around the globe. For many years, the lists have provided rankings of the fifty places on Earth where it is most costly to be a follower of Christ. The 2020 list continues to be topped by North Korea, followed by nations like Afghanistan, Somalia, Libya, and Pakistan as the four countries of the most sustained Christian persecution.[6] Worldwide, an estimated 260 million Christians suffer for the name, ranging from living under government surveillance (as, for example, in China) to social ostracism and acts of violence and torture, often resulting in death. Tribulation and persecution on account of the word of

---

5. A second possible allusion to the Old Testament here may be to Mal 3:16—4:2.

6. Open Doors, "World Watch List."

The Kingdom Admits of Opposition

the kingdom not only remains a reality today, but is at an all-time high. For just as some decide to believe in the message of Jesus and are sown into the world as the "good seed," others decide to oppose it and to harass those who profess Christ.[7] Open persecution and intimidation identify one of the two main methods the devil employs to wage war against the kingdom of Christ. Satan does not only snatch away the word sown in many hearts (Matt 13:19). He actively opposes the people of God and seeks to destroy or silence them. When this happens, Christians face the decision: Am I going to take flight or am I going to fight? Perseverance in the face of persecution and crisis is the way of the cross and the way in which the true confessor is separated from the hypocrite. Conflict will reveal what a person is made of and where both one's heart and treasure are (Matt 6:21).

So the story invites consideration of the church as a corporate entity. Although not of the world, she is still in the world, and is therefore included in the global scenario portrayed in the parable. The conflict between wheat and tares runs right through the body of Christ. No Christian ought to be perplexed at the reality of prolonged struggle with the community of faith, as counterproductive as such feuds may seem to be. Professing believers at variance with each other is never a desirable scenario, but one must not fail to see that the epic clash of good and evil will also be revealed in the church as a battleground, not merely in the world at large. Not only was Jesus crucified by his own people at the gates of Jerusalem, but "sons of the evil one" are also sown in Christ's churches. In so many ways, our attitude toward the local body of Christ betrays our true allegiances. Our love for Christ is only as great as our love for his bride. The apostle Paul hints at the concept of the church as a place of "two seeds" in his words to the Corinthians: "I hear that there are divisions among you. And I believe it in part, for there must be factions among you in order that those who are genuine among you may be recognized" (1 Cor 11:18–19). Samuel John Stone's hymn from the 1860s expresses the idea

---

7. Note that the identification of the seed has shifted slightly from the word of the kingdom (sower) to the people of the kingdom (weeds).

Old and New

poetically: "Though there be those that hate her, and false sons in her pale . . ."[8] The hymn was composed in response to schism and heresy within the churches of South Africa.[9]

If the church is within the overall purview of Jesus' story, the master's words that curb the holy zeal of his servants (angels) who want to uproot the weeds call for some reflection. Has the church no mandate to promote her own purity? As Jesus' commentary indicates, "The harvest is the close of the age" (Matt 13:39); the burning of the weeds symbolizes the final judgment in which good and evil will be finally separated with eternal ramifications. So, when the master denies his servants' desire to take preemptive measures and deal with the problem, his appeal is aimed at the execution of judgment before the appointed time. He is concerned with how and when to solve the conflict created by the present opposition to the kingdom. The score will not be settled before the end, and the judgment belongs to the Son of Man. In the meantime, while the church has no *coercive* power, she has been given *persuasive* power to maintain peace and purity within her own ranks. But church discipline according to God's biblical blueprint and as a vital mark of the true church, whatever form it may take, is not part of the story's scope. It simply affirms that the tug-of-war between the seeds must be expected in the last days. Both seeds will grow together, even within local churches.

The fulcrum of the parable, introduced by the question of the servants to the master, is also interesting for another reason. "Do you want us to go and gather them?" (13:28). The rationale behind the question is entirely logical. The weeds were not sown by the master, and they should therefore be uprooted. But the master instructs his servants not to try to root up the weeds so as not to harm the wheat. He foresees a "mixed" community of both good and bad.[10] He urges restraint and tolerance, assuring the servants

---

8. *Trinity Psalter Hymnal* #404.

9. Both notions come into view in stanza 3: "By schisms rent asunder, by heresies distressed, yet saints their watch are keeping, their cry goes up, 'How long?'"

10. Senior, *Matthew*, 153.

The Kingdom Admits of Opposition

that evil will be dealt with at the end, namely at the time of the harvest.

However, his concern for the wheat in the context of the presence of weeds must be weighed all the more carefully. The master farmer is in full control of the situation and knows where the weeds have come from and how they were sown in his field, as if he had been watching the treachery.[11] While the story itself offers no further clues about God's ultimate purpose in all this, except to establish the eschatological horizon of the final solution to the conflict in the judgment, we are entitled to raise the issue. Assuming a biblical world view, the sabotage of the enemy does not catch God by surprise; rather, the opposition of Satan and his "weeds" has been anticipated and is part of the plot of God's story, his plan for the world. Since the parable's horizon extends all the way to the final judgment, his purposeful design from the beginning to the end lies just beneath the surface of the story. The struggle between the wheat and the weeds, therefore, must have purpose, and the conclusion imposes itself: the kingdom does not only admit of opposition, but the battleground is the appointed sphere in which the good seed must grow. The struggle is not wasted. Rather, it seems to be yet another (perhaps much ignored) secret of the kingdom. Viewed in this light, the parable of the weeds teaches perseverance.

There is perseverance of the master himself who knows how to wait patiently for the right season of harvest. All the Bible's teachings on perseverance and patience find their source in God's character. He is perseverant (cf. 1 Tim 1:16; Heb 12:2; 2 Pet 3:9) and has persevered with us his people throughout history.[12] Thus, when the servants are encouraged to be patient *with* the master, we must learn the same lesson and be prepared to persevere with God by our side. As James 5:7 exhorts us with agrarian imagery that aligns well with the parable of the weeds, "Be patient, then, brothers, until the Lord's coming. See how the farmer waits for the land to yield its valuable crop and how patient he is for the autumn and spring rains." But perseverance must "have its full effect" (Jas 1:4).

---

11. Cf. Kistemaker, *The Parables of Jesus*, 40.
12. Cf. Welch, *Depression*, 80.

Old and New

The end product suggests a refining process: "Then the righteous will shine like the sun" is an allusion to Daniel 12:3, as mentioned above, and an invitation to consider its context more closely. For 12:2 predicts "a time of trouble, such as never has been." The tribulation of God's people refers to persecution in the last days. Hence, Revelation 7:14 portrays the church triumphant on the far side of judgment day as those "coming out of the great tribulation." The entire New Testament era is the time of tribulation for the "good seed," because, as the apostle once affirmed, "Through many tribulations we must enter the kingdom of God" (Acts 14:22).

So the struggle is designed to refine us and ultimately to separate the wheat from the weeds. The struggle is the means by which the separation is beginning to take shape until it is final and eternal in the end. And as Paul said, the opposition of the enemy, far from succeeding in destroying the good seed, serves the purpose of preparing God's people for "an eternal weight of glory beyond all comparisons" (2 Cor 4:17). The pattern of suffering, victory, and glorification is the pattern of Jesus Christ, who himself was made perfect through suffering (Heb 2:10). He did this for us, but we have need of it, too. God wants to share himself with his people in the fullest sense, and this cannot be unless he also reduces us, humbles us, and makes us rely on him alone in everything. We cannot be filled with the fullness of God in Christ without first being emptied or losing what holds us back. Faith teaches us that suffering, conflict, and opposition are God's design to ready us for what is coming, as it was with Christ. Faith therefore also acts on this conviction by persevering, even when the world looks grim and hope has all but vanished because God appears to be in hiding. C. S. Lewis is right in pointing out that such perseverance against the odds of our own will, weakness, and what appears to be a hopeless situation is a weapon that Satan has reason to fear. Lewis makes this observation in a warning from the demon Screwtape to his apprentice Wormwood: "Our cause is never more in danger when a human, no longer desiring, but still intending, to do our Enemy's will, looks around upon a universe from which every trace of him seems to have vanished, and asks why he has been forsaken,

The Kingdom Admits of Opposition

and still obeys."[13] The perseverance of the saints is an omen of the devil's doom. So the parable of the weeds teaches us that the kingdom must and will be opposed and urges perseverance.

The conclusion is also suggested by the next two parables, the mustard seed and the leaven. Without dwelling on any details now, both are parables of growth. The parable of the weeds placed in this particular context of stories of growth intimates that the role of the enemy and the "sons of the evil one" is ultimately to test and grow God's people through hardship and persecution. This conclusion is driven by the fact that Matthew placed the interpretation of the weeds *after* the two parables of growth so as to create a frame around them. Opposition and growth are not contradictory. Rather, suffering is fertilizer, the critical ingredient to promote sanctification and, in the end, the perfection of the people of God.

Jesus therefore knew that there would be not only a delay in the coming of the kingdom in power and glory, but that the path of his disciples would be the path of his cross. There will be continuing suffering on account of the good news of the kingdom until the end. The faith of believers will be tested severely, but the church will grow amidst the trials and pain, as Jesus will also emphasize later in Matthew's Gospel (16:18–19). The delay of the final judgment, which was commonly expected to occur at the Messiah's coming, is for the express purpose of growth of the good seed. It is the Father's will that his children manifest their faith in the conflict that Daniel had predicted (Dan 9–12) and that reached its first climax in the crucifixion of the Lord (Dan 9:26), but the outcome is never in doubt (Dan 12:1–4). Judging is the prerogative of the Son of Man, who therefore takes to himself (once again) God's very own business.[14] This echoes one point of the previous chapter. In the parable of the sower, Jesus assumed the role of God as the sower of the word. No prophet ever made such a sweeping claim, and no one ever has since. Here, the scenario is the same. Jesus applies God's prerogative to himself and claims that he is doing what the Scriptures say God himself would do. He will separate the

---

13. Lewis, *The Screwtape Letters*, 39.
14. Hill, *The Gospel of Matthew*, 235–37.

Old and New

human race and decide who will enter his glorious kingdom and who will not.[15] His divinity lies just beneath the surface of the text.

Many centuries have passed, and the epic struggle continues. Churches have been planted, have grown, and many have disappeared over time, but the work always moved forward in places—through the tribulation that Jesus taught, not the least as implied by this parable. One telling example relates to the Evangelical Church of France. Antoine Court was only nineteen years old when in 1714 he moderated a synod of nine persecuted Reformed Christian churches. Despite outright violence and intimidation by both Rome and the French government under Louis XV, they remained faithful to God's word.[16] In the midst of dire circumstances, they cultivated the reading and study of Scripture, created a new church constitution and led a sober life of faith and prayer. The pastors and members of these Reformed churches lived under the constant threat of death, and all the attendees of the 1714 Synod except Court paid for their commitment to the gospel with their blood in subsequent years. Nevertheless, the church endured, because it was not "their" church, but the church of Jesus Christ, the good seed of the kingdom in this world. It will continue to grow, and there will be a rich harvest in the end. The building of the church of Christ has now lasted for two thousand years, and we are still here. The costs so far have been enormous. We are fellow workers, but not the architect or client. It is the Lord Jesus, and what he has begun will one day be completed according to his unique blueprint. As the prophet Habakkuk once said amidst grim circumstances:

> Though the fig tree should not blossom, nor fruit be on the vines, the produce of the olive fail and the fields yield no food, the flock be cut off from the fold and there be no herd in the stalls, yet I will rejoice in the LORD; I will take joy in the God of my salvation. GOD, the Lord is my strength. (Hab 3:17–19)

---

15. Cf. also Blomberg, *Interpreting the Parables*, 320.

16. They referred to the leaders of the Reformed churches of France as "preachers and elders of the assemblies in the wilderness."

The Kingdom Admits of Opposition

Habakkuk taught his heart to rejoice in the Lord's unfaltering design when he could have resigned in misery and despair. We must make the same decision in our mind and heart, and our attitude will follow suit. In this way, we can escape the spell of darkness. One look at God changes everything. It is like a father who says to his kids, "Now it's time for joy!" As if one could stipulate joy! But this is the secret behind the imperative. God has ordered joy as the antidote to despair irrespective of our circumstances, and we can therefore also tap into it by his grace, because he gives both to will and to do of his good pleasure. No matter the burden, how great our problems, how little time, how pressing the challenges may be—we must train ourselves to rejoice in the Lord. His goodness meets us in a thousand and more ways, as in his creation, in a conversation with a friend, in family time, and even in a dog. "Yet, I will rejoice in the LORD!"

Joy in the midst of conflict has everything to do with hearing. The interpretation of the parable of the weeds closes with the same exhortation as the sower: "He who has ears to hear, let him hear!" Hearing is a lost art in our culture; few have the patience to practice it well, but our own perseverance in patience depends on proper hearing of God's word. A common phenomenon these days is people walking, driving, and running with headphones, listening to their own tunes and favorite pundits, but they are cut off from the world around them. If you speak to them, they will not hear you. I cannot help but wonder whether this is not also an acted metaphor of how we have shut out God lest we should hear him speak to us.

4

The Kingdom's Humble Seed and Miraculous Growth

SETI IS SHORTHAND FOR "Search for Extraterrestrial Intelligence," a collective term for exploring the possibility of life on distant planets. We entertain speculations of "exoplanets," worlds in far-flung solar systems that resemble our own, with an atmosphere that supports life. To this present day, no such planet has actually been found, although conjectures run high about Kepler-62f, Kepler-186f, and Kepler-442b. New candidates are added constantly. These planets orbit stars thousands of light years away in what is called a circumstellar habitable zone, and are believed to sustain conditions comparable to those of "Mother Earth." The astronomer Carl Sagan led the way among a group of scientists in the 1960s who were decidedly optimistic (if not euphoric) about the possibility of life on distant planets. But half a century ago, scientists possessed a rather limited database with regards to the parameters necessary for extraterrestrial life. A planet that supports life required a certain kind of solar system (or star) and needed to be located in the right range of distance from its sun (or suns). Given the vast number of galaxies in the universe, Sagan calculated that

The Kingdom's Humble Seed and Miraculous Growth

there would be a wealthy number of planets that could support life. All we needed to do is find them and celebrate the discovery.

Today, we monitor electromagnetic radiation for signs of transmissions from other worlds and scan the skies for messages from alien civilizations. The Keck telescopes near the summit of Mauna Kea on Hawaii at an altitude of over 4100 meters allows us to observe and scan the universe with unprecedented power and precision, as space telescopes take our ability to view distant galaxies to "Andromeda heights." But for all the concerted efforts, not even a hint of extraterrestrial life or a habitable planet has been confirmed. At the same time, scientists continue to add to the list of conditions necessary to sustain planetary life, having come to a greater understanding of the most delicate balance of life on planet Earth. Indeed, the variables required for life have exploded in number, causing the possibility of even a single planet in the universe being able to support life to shrink dramatically.

For apart from the ongoing quest for new worlds, life on planet Earth itself, by any statistical measures, is so improbable that it should not exist at all. Yet, here we are! The odds stacked against life and a proper environment on Earth are scientifically so enormous, or rather, overwhelming, that our existence must be declared a wonder, a tremendous miracle in and of itself. The exact size of the Earth is of the essence. With just a little more gravity (mass and size), toxic gases like methane and ammonia would remain on the Earth's surface for us to inhale. But if the Earth were smaller, with less gravity, water vapor would evaporate, thus depleting the Earth's water resources over time. And even the properties of water itself are a veritable conundrum, in that water's frozen state weighs less than its liquid state. $H2O$ becomes less dense and therefore lighter when frozen. This contradicts the way other chemical compounds behave. A gas is less dense than a liquid, and a liquid less dense than a solid, as the molecules move closer together from one state to the next. But water does not fit with this otherwise universal principle. It follows its own rule, as ice is lighter than water in liquid form and therefore floats. But this unexpected property is crucial, for if water became denser in its frozen state, then all the freshwater bodies, including rivers, would be frozen from the bottom up and make the survival of aquatic life in cold conditions impossible.

Then again, the duration of an Earth day is twenty-four hours, due to the planet's speed of rotation. If periods of light and darkness were either longer or shorter (depending on rotation speed), it would result in monumental climatological changes, making a stable environment impossible. We may add to this the size, relative distance from the Earth, and singularity of the moon,[1] accounting for the ebb and flow of oceans due to the moon's gravitational field. Since the vast majority of all marine life is found in the shallow nearshore regions of the oceans, the tide is crucial in replenishing coastal waters that allow life to flourish.

Life is a wonder, and this leads us to the parable of the mustard seed.[2] Obviously, in using the story, Jesus has no interest in scientific data, as he only observes a common agrarian phenomenon, but in his own way he draws attention to a small slice (shall I say, speck) of the great wonder of life on Earth. How is it that the burial of a proverbially tiny seed[3] produces such a sizable plant, large enough to be compared to a tree?[4] Bailey points out that the diminutive size of the mustard seed compared to the sheer size of the mature organism was indeed proverbial in ancient Jewish culture.[5] Given the size of the pip, the process should take a long time, but the plant grows exceedingly fast, reaching its full size in just a few years. The parable celebrates the wonder of the mustard seed's astonishing growth.[6]

---

1. In our solar system, every planet with a moon has more than one, except Earth.

2. This is the only parable called a parable *of the kingdom* by all three Synoptic authors (Matt 13:31–32; Mark 4:30–32; Luke 13:18–19).

3. The mustard seed measures about 1.5 to 3 millimeters in diameter (0.04 to 0.08 inches).

4. Thomson claims that a mustard plant can grow to a height of over twelve feet. Thomson, *The Land and the Bible*, 183.

5. Bailey, "The Parable of the Mustard Seed," 453.

6. Hultgren, *The Parables of Jesus*, 395.

The Kingdom's Humble Seed and Miraculous Growth

But before we turn to its two main aspects that concern the kingdom, it is worthwhile to consider how Jesus transformed the metaphor of sowing seed. It has remained a staple throughout the first three of the seven parables in Matthew 13. From this point on, Jesus will employ domestic and commercial images to illustrate the nature of God's kingdom. The parable of the mustard seed thus brings closure to the first half of the textual complex.

In the parable of the sower, the seed is the word. The parable of the weeds identifies the seed and the plants that grow from it as the people of God and their enemies. Now, the seed that is sown is itself the kingdom of heaven, viewed in its entirety. This perspective of totality would naturally include the notions of the first two parables, namely the word and the people of the kingdom ("sons of the kingdom," 13:38). Moreover, as we move from one parable to the next, the stories, sharing the imagery of the field, seed, and sowing, work together in collaboration in a funneling trajectory. In the first parable, the sower sows the seed, and there are four types that Jesus characterizes in terms of their reaction to the message of the kingdom. In the second parable with agrarian imagery, we have two types of plants that grow from the seeds that are sown by two respective sowers, God's children and the children of the enemy. Finally, in the parable of the mustard seed, the sower sows but a single seed (and a rather tiny one) to set in motion a staggering success story. The miniscule seed grows into a massive tree. So the reader of this triad of parables is led along a narrowing path of four objects, then two, and finally only one object of a kind to consider. When seen in concert, the parables of sowers and seeds create a funneling effect with a trajectory that reduces to singularity.

The ultimate focus on a singular seed and plant representing the kingdom of heaven holds two related notions: Small or rather humble beginnings and astounding growth,[7] illustrated

---

7. Significantly, Luke 13:18-19 omits the reference to the plant becoming "larger than all the garden plants" (Matt 13:32). Thus, along with Mark's version (Mark 4:30-32), Matthew places more stress on the contrast between humble beginnings and unexpected outcomes. Cf. Hultgren, *The Parables of Jesus*, 400.

49

by picturing the tree becoming a host for all kinds of birds. As for humble beginnings, Jesus draws attention to the well-known diminutive size of the mustard seed. It holds little or no promise in itself, which makes the finished product appear all the more amazing. Did Jesus have a specific referent in mind when he spoke of this elfin seed? In John 12:23–25, he refers to his crucifixion and death as the burial of a seed that will eventually bear much fruit. It is almost certain that Jesus thought of his own sacrifice for the sins of his people as the humble beginning of the kingdom that is here rendered as the sowing of the mustard seed. Isaiah had predicted that the advent of the Redeemer would take many by surprise on account of its self-effacing and coy appeal: "As many were astonished at you—his appearance was so marred beyond human semblance and his form beyond that of the children of mankind ... For he grew up before him like a young plant, and like a root out of dry ground; he had no form or majesty that we should look at him" (Isa 52:14; 53:2). He would not be much look at—like a tiny mustard seed that is hard to see. Looks can be so deceiving! Who would think that the kingdom of heaven begins with a man decried as a heretic and a criminal hanging on a cross?

This conclusion draws support from the parable's context. As we noted earlier, Matthew 13 rises from the first climax of opposition against Jesus, reached by the end of chapter 12. The block of seven parables and interpretive sayings answers the question that is looming over the antagonism the King faced by his own people. Both the sower and the weeds confirm that the coming of the kingdom of God is only partially realized and therefore also admits of hostility for the time being. The mustard seed sown in the earth offers an allusion to the end of Jesus' ministry, when hostility would reach its culminating expression in his torturous death and subsequent burial. The fact that the mustard seed is sown "in the field" (Matt 13:31) may in this regard be considered a deliberate, audible echo of the parable of the weeds, with its setting of the field as a place of conflict between the sons of the kingdom and the sons of the evil one. So, when the mustard seed is sown into the *field*, with the previous story still in mind, the location of the sowing can be

The Kingdom's Humble Seed and Miraculous Growth

construed as a hostile environment in which growth is unexpected or at least hampered.[8]

Seen in this light, the parable addresses the disappointment that Jesus' audience must have felt. Everyone expected impressive things and overwhelming events that accompanied the coming of the King, but the reality of Jesus' ministry would have been perceived as deflating on account of such divided responses, not to speak of the ultimate scandal of the crucifixion.[9] The mustard seed taught Jesus' contemporaries and teaches us not to be deceived or confused by size. Nevertheless, for the time being, not a few would have been shocked by the idea of such inconsequential and lowly origination. Israel had been humbled for hundreds of years and presently lived under the thumb of Roman imperial rule. No king had sat on David's throne for six long centuries, during which the people of God had paid crushing taxes to foreign monarchs, although they had once been set free from slavery to live only under God's rule. Surely the advent of the promised Messiah would not—could not—unfold like a Cinderella tale with unlikely success, never mind the final outcome! Moses was sent to Egypt and forced Pharaoh to his knees with ten prodigious, overwhelming plagues from heaven, and the coming of the Davidic scion was therefore expected to be no inferior display of divine authority than the bared arm of the Lord during the exodus. But Jesus knew that his way of the paradoxical servant of the Lord was the way of the cross and humiliation, a path that led through a shameful death and burial like a lowly mustard seed, and only by humbling himself to the point of the cross for his chosen people would the kingdom's incredible growth potential be set in motion and eventually realized in full.

In the same way, growth in both the church and the individual believer occurs only where there is also a humble beginning,

---

8. Only Matthew has the seed sown in the field, which may suggest a deliberate anaphoric reference to the setting of the previous parables. Mark describes the seed as "sown upon the soil" ("earth," Greek *ge*, 4:31), and Luke writes of the seed as one that a man took and "threw into his garden" (13:19).

9. Cf. Wenham, *The Parables of Jesus*, 54.

a reduction, and a death to self in a thousand installments. Jesus' axiomatic saying encapsulates the cardinal growth principle of the gospel: "Everyone who exalts himself will be humbled, and he who humbles himself will be exalted" (Luke 14:11; cf. 1 Pet 5:6). Our greatest victories in the Christian life walk on shattered legs and are wrought through brokenness and humility, a lesson as counterintuitive as it is hard to learn, but with wonderful divine promise. God never fails to surprise us by his grace.

Why does it have to be so? Why does God's reign arrive with such humble beginnings? There may be more than one good answer to this mystery of the kingdom. But the apostle Paul highlighted the essence of God's good news logic in Romans 4:16–25 in terms of two divine attributes that ultimately function as the promoters of God's glory and fame, namely grace and power:

> That is why it depends on faith, in order that the promise may rest on grace and be guaranteed to all his offspring—not only to the adherent of the law but also to the one who shares the faith of Abraham, who is the father of us all, as it is written, "I have made you the father of many nations"—in the presence of the God in whom he believed, who gives life to the dead and calls into existence the things that do not exist. In hope he believed against hope, that he should become the father of many nations, as he had been told, "So shall your offspring be." He did not weaken in faith when he considered his own body, which was as good as dead (since he was about a hundred years old), or when he considered the barrenness of Sarah's womb. No distrust made him waver concerning the promise of God, but he grew strong in his faith as he gave glory to God, fully convinced that God was able to do what he had promised. That is why his faith was "counted to him as righteousness." But the words "it was counted to him" were not written for his sake alone, but for ours also. It will be counted to us who believe in him who raised from the dead Jesus our Lord, who was delivered up for our trespasses and raised for our justification.

From the beginning, God worked with unlikely candidates. Abraham "was as good as dead" (4:19), and Sarah barren, and yet

The Kingdom's Humble Seed and Miraculous Growth

from this geriatric couple God built the nation of Israel. In a similar way, God raised Christ from the dead to enthrone him on his right hand. He is the seed that is sown in dishonor to grow into the kingdom tree, home to every kind of bird. So God shows himself as the One "who gives life to the dead and calls into existence the things that do not exist" (4:17). The kingdom has a humble beginning to exclude any kind of boasting on our part. Abraham and Sarah could only point to God's grace for the *Wunderkind* Isaac, the son of promise. We have a part in Christ's kingdom through no accomplishment of our own. The lowly mustard seed is a token of the dynamics of God's grace. On the other hand, the stunning growth rate of the plant is a simile of divine power, God's miracle of life and of making his kingdom flourish from virtually nothing. He makes it grow from nothing, because only he can, and this is his signature, to call things into existence from nil. His glory is exalted by both his grace and power. So there may be a small beginning, but God's strange work will live up to the glory of his name, as did the original creation *ex nihilo*. In this way, the parable of the mustard seed is intended to encourage all who respond to and share the message of the kingdom. Hostility and opposition will not remain forever, but God and his people have the last laugh. Never doubt God's grace and power to work through you, no matter how inadequate you feel, but consider the mustard seed. Jesus says that the seed outgrows all the garden plants to become a tree.

The amazing process is further illustrated by his reference to the birds that nest in its branches. The Greek term "πετεινὰ" (birds) introduces an element of irony and offers a touch of refined literary closure to the three parables of sowing and seeds. The parable of the sower began with "the birds" (Matt 13:4) devouring the seed sown by the wayside. The birds are now peacefully nesting in the branches of the kingdom tree and furnish the final and indelible impression of the three related stories about the reign of God. Isaiah 54:1–3 describes the growth of the kingdom in terms of a tent that is in need of a dramatic enlargement because the gentile nations will become Israel's possession. Again, Isaiah 55:5 addresses the son of David, who is given the following promise:

"Behold, you shall call a nation that you do not know, and a nation that did not know you shall run to you, because of the LORD your God, and of the Holy One of Israel, for he has glorified you." The "nation" here is a reference to people previously excluded from God's covenant with Israel. No longer. As 42:6 already predicts, the Anointed King and Servant of the LORD will be given as a covenant for the people, "a light for the nations."

So the birds nesting in the tree could well be a veiled way of speaking of the gentile nations finding a home among Israel in God's kingdom through Jesus Christ. The birds of the heavens living in the branches of a mighty tree is a known Old Testament motif depicting the nations of the world.[10] Daniel 4:12 describes the glory of the Babylonian Empire with the help of the tree image, with birds nesting in its branches. An even closer parallel to Jesus' parable of the kingdom is found in Ezekiel 17:23-24. The text foresees the future of the messianic age as a cedar tree growing from a tiny sprig broken off a branch that becomes the host of every kind of bird: "I will plant it; it will produce branches and bear fruit and become a splendid cedar. Birds of every kind will nest in it; they will find shelter in the shade of its branches" (Ezek 17:24). Ezekiel's vision of the cedar sprig is the Old Testament counterpart to the mustard seed, not the least because it expressly anticipates the messianic reign coming through a son of David. Yet, Jesus' parable, which assembles a collage of prophetic themes, also pushes the boundaries of Ezekiel's picture on both ends via comparisons: The seedling is "the smallest," and the grown plant is the "largest of all the garden plants."

In both cases, though, the copious bird life of the tree symbolizes the international proportions of the kingdom.[11] So the extensive growth of the tiny mustard seed contains the Old Testament promise of the inclusion of the Gentiles in the covenant of grace,[12]

---

10. Cf. Bailey's comments in "The Parable of the Mustard Seed," 455.

11. Hagner, "Matthew's Parables of the Kingdom," 114.

12. "Out of the most insignificant beginnings, invisible to the human eye, God creates his mighty kingdom, which embraces all people of the world." Jeremias, *The Parables of Jesus*, 149.

The Kingdom's Humble Seed and Miraculous Growth

as the prophets of Israel had predicted.[13] "Many shall come from the east and the west and recline at table with Abraham, Isaac, and Jacob, in the kingdom of heaven" (Matt 8:11). Jesus' allusion to this Old Testament motif shows that he knew his mission was consistent with God's prophetic promises for the world, even though he remained misunderstood among his own people. He saw that what happened in his present ministry in embryonic form carried the DNA of the promise of the future triumph of his rule. God's intervention through him guaranteed the great ending. The mustard seed in particular shows that Jesus thought of himself as the seedling of an unbroken organic process between "now" and "then."[14] The by-all-appearances insignificant royal seed would grow not through any worldly forces but through God's miraculous power until the process is complete and the kingdom will be unveiled in triumphant glory. The parable thus states one of the great "secrets of the kingdom" (13:11). If life itself is a miracle, how much more the growth of God's rule from a "dead seed."

The organic image of the seed and the tree places us too in this royal process of growth.[15] We exist and operate in a constant, unbroken spectrum between "today" and "tomorrow," when the kingdom will appear in splendor. Whatever we do today in the name of the Lord carries the promise of a glorious future because God's power is at work especially in humble circumstances, humble beginnings, just as his power is perfected in weakness (cf. 2 Cor 12:9). Every kind gesture, every act of generosity, especially in adverse circumstances, are mustard seeds that can grow into trees for birds to nest in. Every act of goodness and love is like a rock that is thrown into the water to produce ripples that spread outward in circular fashion until they meet the shore. We lowly people are called and blessed indeed! Therefore, the plot of the

---

13. As indicated above, Jesus' image of the mustard seed seems even more conscious of the humble beginnings of the flourishing kingdom. No sprig that has at least a trace of the promise of a mighty cedar, the mustard seed has no appeal and awaits an even more dramatic transformation.

14. Cf. Schnackenburg, *God's Rule*, 159.

15. Cf. Beasley-Murray, *Jesus and the Kingdom of God*, 124.

story continues to unfold in countless applications in everyday life, as the power of God breaks into our world in unobtrusive but very real ways. The process is underway, and it cannot be reversed or stopped; the seed has been sown, the plant is growing. We are part of the process through faith in the gospel of the mustard seed, and the final victory is divinely guaranteed.

The scenario may look like a blind person sitting in a public concourse who reads from the Gospels of Christ. He does not know whether anyone sits with him or not, but he keeps on reading out loud from his braille Bible with embossed paper, slowly scanning page after page with his fingers. When he stops deciphering the sign language, there is a hand gently shoving him. "Read on!" So he reads on. The blind man can even read at night because he needs no light. Jesus is using him who is of no consequence to the many ignorant passersby in ways that only the Lord can see, and with eternal glorious ramifications. What a sight it will be when his strange work is seen in the blazing light of the age to come!

5

The Kingdom's Hidden Growth

THE PARABLE OF THE leaven has been placed like a hinge. As the fourth and central piece in the complex of seven, it forms the connective tissue between the first three and the following three stories. Its overt focus on the growth of the kingdom provides a close tie to the parable of the mustard seed, which also includes the language of "taking" (Matt 13:31, 33) to introduce the main action (i.e., sowing seed and hiding yeast, respectively). In addition, the leaven is the last parable spoken by Jesus to the crowds by the Sea of Galilee. From here, the public setting gives way to Jesus' private instruction to the disciples in the remaining three parables.[1] On the other hand, the well-known domestic scene described in this parable serves as a preface to the second half of the set of seven, where we see a lucky fellow stumbling upon a treasure, an expert merchant of pearls in the marketplace, and a crew of seasoned fishermen going about their routine business. The language of "hiding"[2] also creates a strong literary link with the following tale of the "hidden" treasure, and perhaps a less obvious nexus with the

---

1. Hagner, "Matthew's Parables of the Kingdom," 115.
2. Hiding yeast in a batch of dough was the customary practice in baking. Cf. Bailey, "The Parable of the Leavening Process" 61–71.

search for an elusive pearl that is only waiting to be found.[3] Beyond this, the parable of the leaven uses the motif of *fullness* ("until it was *all* leavened," 13:33), which is present in all the remaining stories and so forms a common denominator. Accordingly, the lucky fellow sells "all" his belongings, as does the merchant hitting paydirt (πάντα, 13:44, 46),[4] and the mariners sort out fish of "all" kinds (παντὸς, 13:47) when their dragnet is full. In this way, the leaven has been placed purposefully as the literary intersection between the two halves of the discourse, having things in common with both the previous and the following matter.

Because the leavening metaphor is employed in several texts of the Old Testament to portray the corrupting effects of evil or sin, a number of predominantly dispensational commentators have argued that leaven here also pictures the corrupting influence of evil in the current church age before God establishes his messianic kingdom at the commencement of the millennium.[5] But this approach falters on several points. To begin with, a most basic hermeneutical principle is that words and phrases must be interpreted in their proper context. Leaven may be a symbol of evil or sin in *some* biblical passages (cf. Exod 34:25; Lev 2:11), but this does not force the conclusion that it has the same connotation in Matthew 13. The leaven's close relation to the mustard seed strongly suggests that, like the seed that is sown in the soil, the fermenting agent that is hidden in the dough represents something that God does to promote his kingdom. After all, Jesus' introductory formula ("The kingdom of heaven is like . . .") links the scene to the reign of God, not the reign of sin in the present age.[6] In any case, the reference to leaven is hardly intended to point to bad things but the great effects that are brought about by an insignificant, secret ingredient, a notion well-aligned with the previous story of sowing seed. The

---

3. Both the parable of the hidden treasure and the parable of the pearl share the vocabulary of "finding" (cf. 13:44, 46).

4. Even though 13:33 uses a different Greek term than 13:44, 46, 47, the theme of fullness or inclusiveness is notable in all four cases.

5. As, for example Touissant, *Behold Your King*, 182.

6. See also Hagner, "Matthew's Parables of the Kingdom," 115.

The Kingdom's Hidden Growth

mustard seed and the leaven placed side by side are meant to have a reinforcing effect on each other, providing slightly different perspectives on the same truth about the coming of the kingdom, and this harmony of the twin parables is wrecked if leaven represents the growing influence of sin in the world.

Another feature of the leaven that strengthens the link with the mustard seed is that, like the seed, the leaven must "die" (or "be buried") in the dough in order to have its astounding effect.[7] The fermenting agent must first be "entombed" in the lump. So this notion could constitute another veiled reference to the death of Jesus Christ, or rather, more generally, the necessity of sacrifice for the kingdom to have influence and to flourish. The nature of Jesus' ministry terminating on a cross in Jerusalem was at once revealing but also concealing the true power of God, and it was this hidden reality that furnished the matrix from which God's reign has emerged and grown, to be seen in glory eventually. The process is completely independent of man's control, like leaven that leavens a lump without human intervention. God is the one who determines the course of events that will culminate in the total triumph of his glorious reign. Therefore, rather than seeing the leaven as a symbol of evil that runs its sinister course and dominates the church age until Christ's return,[8] the scene offers a positive view of the unobtrusive growth of God's reign in the world.

There may be, however, one sense in which the fairly traditional association of leaven with evil can be retained at least indirectly, namely as an element of shock. Many, if not all, of Jesus' parables were pregnant with such an element of shock, and this may be one, too. Jesus knew that leaven had a bad press in Judaism,[9] and thus may have employed the metaphor to conjure what was distasteful to many contemporary, respectable Jews. It would have been unpalatable for them to hear the kingdom of God being likened to leaven, not to mention a woman as the main character of the simile. First-century Jewish culture was dominated by

---

7. See Gerhardsson, "The Seven Parables of Matthew 13," 23.
8. Touissant, *Behold Your King*, 182.
9. Green, *Matthew for Today*, 138.

males, and the status of women was inferior.[10] Jesus' use of a female as an illustration for God's reign was countercultural, as was his elevation of women in many other cases.[11] And yet, is this not how Jesus and his rabble of untaught fishermen, women, tax collectors, and notorious sinners seemed to those of religious pedigree, a trail of politically incorrect choices that led all the way to the scandal of the cross? There is a sense in which God's *modus operandi* is always good for a healthy surprise. The kingdoms of the world have bears, lions, bulls, and birds of prey as their emblems and insignia, and they are shown on flags and crests. Human history documents just how well we have chosen them, for the kingdoms of this world often act like predators and ravenous birds, taking what does not belong to them and killing in the process. God rejects our fascination with images of muscular, proud beasts, which also serve as the gods of the nations, from Marduk, the horned bull-god of ancient Babylon, to the charging bull of Wall Street in our brave new world. God raises a flag that shows no beast but a slain lamb as the sign of his kingdom. At face value, this is deplorably bad publicity, bad marketing. In the concert of the voices and images that are hoisted and amplified through the media in the public marketplace, the image and message of the cross seems to get lost. The kingdom remains hidden. Still, the offense of leaven used to portray the growth of the kingdom is not likely to have been lost on Jesus' listeners.

But as a parable of growth, the leaven forms a pleasing match with the mustard seed, notwithstanding a new and challenging nuance of the concept of the kingdom's expansion. For while the previous story puts the accent on *ex*tensive growth, the leaven has its center of gravity in the *in*tensive growth of the kingdom. Spiritual growth does not necessarily appear to the naked eye. It is hidden and unobtrusive. The kingdom operates according to

10. Cf. McLaughlin, *Confronting Christianity*, 136–39.
11. Luke's Gospel makes the most of this aspect of Jesus' life and ministry. As Luke 7:36–50 and 8:1–3 show, Jesus' entourage included many women, something that first-century rabbis would not have countenanced. Likewise, in Luke 10:42, Mary assumes a traditionally male role, sitting at Jesus' feet with his disciples (cf. also Luke 21:1–4).

The Kingdom's Hidden Growth

an internal force that remains undetectable to the observer until the batch rises. But the effect of Christ's reign, though to some extent concealed, will nonetheless be comprehensive in the end. The leavening process reveals that there is something at work and living below, something obstinate and insuperable, though largely unnoticed. The ferment is as dynamic and pervasive as the reign and activity of God, and it cannot be stopped once set in motion.[12] So the process depicted in the scene is a token of the supreme and invincible power of God at work—but, for the time being, content to remain in concealment.

The kingdom of heaven as the reign of Christ or God is a dynamic concept. In the present age, his domain is spiritual, not territorial or universal.[13] His word is acknowledged and obeyed only among his followers and within their hearts by faith. So, in contrast to the theocratic mode of the kingdom of Israel under the old covenant, the reign of Christ has no present territorial claim on land in this old creation.[14] Jesus himself once said, "The kingdom of God is not coming with signs to be observed, nor will they say, 'Look, here it is!' or 'there!' for behold, the kingdom of God is in your midst [or 'within you']" (Luke 17:20–21). Yes, the kingdom will one day come in overwhelming power and glory, when the

---

12. Hunter, *Interpreting the Parables*, 44.

13. While the reign of God has always been spiritual, there is a difference in its manifestation during the Old Testament. The kingdom of God used to exist as a veritable territorial domain, with national borders and its capital in Jerusalem. In contrast to Israel's static notion of the Old Testament kingdom, the New Testament idea of the kingdom is indeed less so one of a *kingdom* with a locative sense and more one of God's active *reign* in and through his people, wherever they may be.

14. For this and other, related reasons, spiritual warfare in these last days does not take the form of military conflict. When the kingdom of Israel had a divinely granted territorial claim on land, there was warfare, conflict, and casualties. But under the new covenant, the promise of land for God's people will have to wait until the last day. The establishment of the (territorial) kingdom as a new creation will be preceded by a preemptive act of war on the world in the coming of Christ (Matt 24:29–31; 2 Thess 1:5–9). Unlike the First World War, this last battle truly is "the war to end all wars," ushering in the eternal *shalom* of Christ and his people. The military engagements during the conquest of Canaan were an omen of the great day that is coming.

kingdom of this world will have become the kingdom of our Lord Jesus Christ (Rev 11:15) and all dominion and authority has been subdued for the reign of God to be total. This sudden intervention will at once stake God's territorial claim over all creation. But until that day, the kingdom advances like the spreading yeast. A small amount is hidden in the dough. In its very nature, the yeast changes whatever it touches or comes into contact with. So is the message of the kingdom. It accomplishes what it is sent for and changes people from the inside out. The apostle Paul speaks of this transformation into the image of Christ in 2 Corinthians 3:18: "[We] are being transformed into the same image from one degree of glory to another. For this comes from the Lord who is the Spirit." The interior transformation of a person will be noticeable in the manner of one's life, but for many this will not amount to a convincing proof that Christ's reign has indeed broken in. The evidence remains ambivalent at best to those who demand unassailable authentication before they consider the reign of God a reality to be reckoned with.

By the same token, as Bloomberg observes,[15] the parable is also an antidote to defeatism and a siege mentality in times when the testimony of Jesus appears to fall on deaf ears or seems fruitless. Things are not what they seem, and Christ's followers are not what they seem. Who can forget the horrid image released by the Islamic State in February 2015? Twenty Egyptian Coptic Christian construction workers along with one Ghanaian had been abducted by Muslim terrorists in Libya. The viral post showed the twenty-one men kneeling before hooded figures dressed in black, lined up for execution. The lips of the Christians are moving in silent prayer to God, who appears to have let them down. Where is the red line, the hand of God that keeps, shelters, and preserves? But a rendering of the artist Tony Rezk offered a radical change of perspective on the massacre.[16] The hooded butchers are nowhere to be found, and the twenty-one martyrs are kneeling by themselves. Above them arches an open heaven, and golden crowns are descending

---

15. Blomberg, *Matthew*, 221.
16 Rezk, "Icon of the 21 martyrs of Libya!"

The Kingdom's Hidden Growth

on their heads. But they do not look at the crowns. They are looking to the enthroned Christ, and their faces are radiating with his very own glory. So there is such a thing as a red line, on a different wavelength, in a different reality than we wish to see or can imagine.

Helmut Thielicke (1908–86) once wrote of the hidden nature of the miracle of the kingdom manifest among Christ's disciples. He recounts how he celebrated the Lord's Supper with a few Ovaherero tribal people in Southern Africa. They kneeled on the ground in the middle of a wasteland. The tribal people had never heard of a city called Hamburg, Germany, and Thielicke knew nothing of this remote place of desert shrubs. No one understood a word the other was saying, but when Thielicke signaled the cross with his hand and pronounced the name "Jesus," their dark, weathered faces were beaming. They ate the bread and drank the cup of the Supper despite apartheid still being a present reality in that part of the world. They had never met before and were complete strangers to each other. Social, geographical, and cultural barriers stood between them. But they were embraced by arms not of this world. Thielicke described the effect the scene had on him, saying, "I understood the miracle of the church."[17] Thielicke knew what he was talking about, but to others, this humble, low-key meeting of a handful of religious people in a howling wilderness was almost absurd and would not be indicative of the reign of Christ as a present reality. A strange company indeed, but hardly the kingdom of heaven on earth.

Yet, although the growth of the kingdom flies under the radar and will never make the headlines of the world's media, the true effect of Christ's reign is beyond measure and its consummation overwhelming. For now, he exerts his influence through his word from within, not with outward, visible glory. But the internal changes he works in the hearts of his followers are only preparatory for the grand finale of the unveiling of the kingdom. What appears initially to be of little consequence produces an astonishing, dramatic revelation in the end, a notion that aligns so well with the

---

17. Bunch, *A Guide to Christian Ethics*, 42.

message of the mustard seed. God's strange, sovereign work independent of human will or control will be gloriously vindicated.[18]

The parable closes with a notice of the finale: "until it was all leavened." Just as yeast works until the dough has completely risen and has been permeated throughout, the reign of Christ will extend to every nation, tongue, and tribe through the progress of the gospel (cf. Matt 24:15), and then the blessing of the kingdom will be universal, as the Old Testament foresaw (Ps 72:19; Dan 2:35). "For the earth will be filled with the knowledge of the glory of the LORD, as the waters cover the sea" (Hab 2:4).

The hiddenness of the kingdom is yet another aspect of Jesus' teaching that would have been puzzling and even confounding to his disciples. Yes, indeed, the small beginnings together with the hidden nature of God's domain were a tough pill to swallow for his contemporaries, who expected clear and unmistakable conditions, a final settling of the score, and the vindication of God's throne over the world from the coming of the Messiah. But Jesus knew that just as yeast takes time to interpenetrate and raise the dough, so also the kingdom advances over time and in inconspicuous ways to issue in its ultimate triumph.[19] If Jesus was not known by his own people (John 1:11), then his disciples, commissioned with the same gospel of peace, cannot expect to be recognized and celebrated in the world like mendacious prosperity preachers who ride ostentatiously on the adoration as well as money of the deceived. They may be inhabiting the praises of people now, but the wages of their sin will be paid out in full (2 Pet 2:1–3). As the leaven is hidden, so is the kingdom of God.[20]

But the kingdom will grow among God's people until the work is finished, so Jesus' followers are encouraged to stand firm and to hope for the promised consummation. For the end will come, and there will be no ambiguity about the nature of the kingdom anymore. "At the name of Jesus every knee will bow, in heaven and on earth and under the earth, and every tongue will confess

---

18. Kingsbury, *Matthew 13*, 86.
19. Kingsbury, *Matthew 13*, 87.
20. Hultgren, *The Parables of Jesus*, 408.

The Kingdom's Hidden Growth

that Jesus Christ is Lord, to the glory of God the Father" (Phil 2:10–11). As believers, we must hold the lesson of the leaven in faith, namely, understanding that the very hiddenness and elusiveness of the kingdom in the present conveys God's expanding rule, for it is indeed what God is doing. The faithful service of Christ's people therefore has eternal significance, though some of it may seem like a desert flower that no one has ever seen. God, however, does see. At the same time, the inauspicious outset and continuing hiddenness of the kingdom also explains the rejection of the word of the kingdom in the hearts of unbelievers. Who will place him- or herself under God's sovereign rule in repentance, when for the time being it fails to impress? His power to save is often invisible to the public eye and never makes the front-page news. The hidden reality of the kingdom is *meant* to have its concealing effect on many, just like Jesus spoke of the blinding effect of his parables (cf. Matt 13:13).

A poem by Eugen Roth[21] captures the hiddenness of the kingdom as an encouragement to all who wait for the consummation, as the unfinished story of God draws us into his final act, the second coming of Jesus Christ, when all will be leavened:

> You know that beyond the forests there are mountains clear and blue. And today heaven is grey and earth is blind. You know that above the clouds so heavy, there stand the stars so bright and beautiful. And today none of all the golden host is seen. And why do you not also believe that the world, a fleeting whiff, cloaks eternity only for today?[22]

Things are not what they seem, and we are not what we seem. "For I know the thoughts that I have for you, declares the LORD, thoughts for peace and not for evil, to give you a future and a hope" (Jer 29:11). There may be people who plot evil against you, and you wish they would not think or speak about you at all, for their thoughts are not for your good or benefit. But God is thinking of you. He is thinking many wonderful thoughts about you, because

---

21. Translated from the German by the author.
22. Freund, *Glücklich Mögest Du Wandern*, 44.

Old and New

he has plans for peace and an expected happy end. David says, "How precious are your thoughts for me, O God! How vast the sum of them! If I would count them, they are more than the sand" (Ps 139:17). Like the woman who bakes bread in the community oven and hides yeast in the lump to set in motion an unstoppable process, we can picture God as an artist who has the idea and the vision, working on a painting. For the present, it is unfinished, and it may not look much, but when it is finished, it is a masterpiece and never stops speaking of his glory. As the old hymn by Heinrich Schenk, *Who Are These Like Stars Appearing*, puts it,

> Who are these like stars appearing, these before God's throne who stand? Each a golden crown is wearing; who are all this glorious band? . . . Who are these of dazzling brightness, these in God's own truth arrayed, clad in robes of purest whiteness, robes whose luster ne'er shall fade, ne'er be touched by time's rude hand? Whence come all this glorious band?[23]

So, again, things are not what they seem, and we are not what we seem. But in the end, what is hidden will be revealed to be admired and marveled at by all creation to the glory of our great God and Savior. For now, the building is concealed by scaffolds and tarps, but the day is coming when it is unveiled—Hallelujah!

---

23. *Tritity Psalter Hymnal* #469.

6

The Kingdom Revealed in Its Full Expression

THE PREVIOUS TWO PARABLES possessed an air of the tentative and the provisional. The present section counters this with its stress on finality. Halfway through the discourse, Jesus' teachings are punctured by Matthew's own commentary (Matt 13:34–35), as he takes inventory of what has been said so far. This brief but significant interlude crystalizes salient truths of three tiers. First of all, Matthew reaffirms that Jesus used parables as didactic illustrations, much the same way that a teacher or preacher would deploy stories to highlight the substance of one's message. Second, he also declares Jesus' method of teaching in parables a fulfillment of Old Testament Scripture (Ps 78:2). The noteworthy quotation from Psalm 78 intimates that, as far as Matthew sees it, Jesus actually speaks with a timeless voice through the writings of the Old Testament prophets, the particular Psalm being exemplary. And third, Jesus' stories have definitive quality because they signal the final stage of God's history of revelation to the world. Whatever used to be hidden is now being revealed. This is what makes this commentary such a balancing follow-up to the parable of the leaven and its governing notion of the kingdom's hiddenness. It is through Jesus that God's final word is spoken to us.¹ Consequently, his unique parables redefine Israel's prophetic deposit of divine truth. Not only do they add the most crucial chapter to the story of God, but through them the whole narrative is retold, redefined, and reoriented, as the focus is squarely on the "Son of Man" (Matt 13:37). His figure is the key that unlocks God's purposes.² The parables of the kingdom are therefore opening a new way of looking at the world and God's plan for it. It is not affording a vista *inconsistent* with God's truth so far revealed, but it is nonetheless groundbreaking in both its depth and resolution. To adopt this novel and subversive worldview by locating oneself in it is the challenge of his stories. The parables require personal identification with the main character Jesus, not merely to enjoy them like a work of fiction, but as a reckless, all-in act of existential surrender to him and his grand story to participate in *both* him and it.

That Jesus made a habit of teaching in parables has already been noted by Matthew in 13:3: "And he told them many things in parables." Yet, his teaching style is now characterized with heightened emphasis: "Indeed, he said *nothing* to them *without* a parable" (13:34).³ Jesus was a wisdom teacher, and the most prized tool in his belt were his signature parables of the kingdom, making him a storyteller par excellence. The most obvious implication of Matthew's motto, "nothing without a parable," is to confront us with Jesus' didactic routine, namely, to keep furnishing stories as illustrations of God's truth about his kingdom. Jesus' stories have often been labelled "earthly stories with heavenly meanings," but this is misleading, a fallacy, for the simple reason that all the kingdom parables are concerned with life on earth, not in heaven.⁴ They do possess illustrative power which is located in the very nature of a story with a *pointe* that captures its particular message.

---

1. The idea of God's definitive word spoken through his Son is, of course, aptly expressed in the opening of the letter to the Hebrews (1:1-2).

2. Cf. Wright, *Jesus and the Victory of God*, 180-81.

3. Emphasis added by author. Matthew even switches from the aorist to the imperfect aspect to stress Jesus' well-established routine of parabolic teaching.

4. Cf. Snodgrass, *Stories with Intent*, 7.

The Kingdom Revealed in Its Full Expression

Concrete pictures as metaphors of ultimate reality lift the hearer above the details of abstract truth and doctrinal instructions (which, of course, have their place). Parables are fictitious but true as they reflect reality from an elevated position. Elevation, in turn, affords a tactical advantage in that it allows us to apprehend the "big picture." The medium or vehicle itself, such as the sowing of a mustard seed or hiding yeast in a lump of dough, may be small and mundane, but its referent is reality or some real process seen from God's control tower. However, Jesus cultivated his method of teaching nothing without a parable not merely for the perfection of didactic brilliance. The parables are analogies that aim to convince, persuade, and convert, namely, to promote a change of heart and life.[5] Like fables, they intend to instill a new way of seeing or making sense of the world in which we live. For, after all, the world is a stage upon which unfolds the mystery of the kingdom of God. As part of this grand unfolding process, Jesus' parables are also a fulfillment of Old Testament prophecies. This brings us to the second tier of truth contained in Matthew 13:34–35.

Matthew's quotation of Psalm 78:2 is remarkable. In both the Hebrew Masoretic Text and the Septuagint (Ps 77:2), there is no mention of things that have been "hidden since the foundation of the world."[6] The psalmist simply announces his intention to speak of ancient truths, "dark sayings from of old." Contrary to the way the text appears in Matthew, he actually does not wish to "hide" them from future generations (78:4), as, in fact, they are well-known, namely "things that we have heard and known, that our fathers have told us" (78:3). He then meanders through the history of Israel during the exodus, all the way to God's choice of David as king of his people. This historical psalm is an object lesson of Israel's rebellion and God's steadfast love and prodigious patience in forgiving and restoring his people time after time. Its ending with David as the chosen king intimates that somehow God will

---

5. Snodgrass, *Stories with Intent*, 9.

6. The first line of the parallel statement from Psalm 78 matches the Septuagint verbatim, whereas the second line is closer, though not identical, to the Hebrew Masoretic Text.

save Israel through a Davidic king. It will not be sin but divine mercy that has the final word, or else the story will have no happy end. But the Psalm does not reveal how this redemption will be realized. It simply raises the specter of hope in pointing to the king without specifying any details. The answer to Israel's dilemma will come through a David, or rather a Davidic scion. With this intimation the Psalm closes and leaves the reader in a spirit of departure and anticipation. It is as if the psalmist finishes his history of Israel with the words, "To be continued," or "David will be back."

The riddle ("dark sayings from of old") of Israel's chronicles of sin will be solved through the king whom God has chosen. Yet Israel had to wait for a millennium to see exactly how. Now Jesus has come, the son of David and God's answer to the ongoing problem of his sin-sick people with a deathwish. He is a teacher of parables, and these his stories tell the people how God will deliver them. While the parables are only accessible through faith for those whom God has blessed with hearing (cf. Matt 13:13), they nevertheless convey the long-awaited reply from heaven. God's reply in the form of the parables pulls together multiple prophetic texts and strands from the Old Testament Scriptures. In this sense, Matthew casts Jesus' customary teaching of parables as the fulfillment not only of Psalm 78 ("This was to fulfill what was spoken by the prophet," 13:35), but as the divine remedy to the continuing tale of Israel's sin and God's covenant faithfulness, which was broached in the conclusion of the "riddle" of David's Psalm, the riddle of the anticipated redemption.

As indicated above, Matthew also introduces a pivotal change to the words of Psalm 78:2.[7] While both the Septuagint (77:2) and the Masoretic Texts (78:2) speak of "parables" and "dark sayings from of old," neither of them portrays the ancient instruction as having been "hidden" from of old ("since the foundation of the world," Matt 13:35). The Psalm actually affirms that the deposit of truth (the history of God and his people) must *not* be hidden

---

7. I assume that he either relied on the Masoretic Text or the Greek version (Septuagint), possibly both. It is, of course, also possible that he worked with a text that we do not know.

The Kingdom Revealed in Its Full Expression

from future generations (Ps 78:4), and there is no talk of things hidden or concealed, waiting to be revealed at some point. Although Matthew is aware of the content and wording of Psalm 78, as his language features the identifiable vocabulary of the Psalm ("parables," "dark saying from of old," "hide"), he combines the words in a new and fresh way to create the notion of a new word from God through Jesus' parables. By speaking of things that have been hidden from the beginning, he gives Jesus' teaching of the kingdom pride of place in the continuing history of God's revelation. His commentary draws attention to the parables as God's final and definitive word to the world. What used to be concealed is now apparent. The missing pieces of the puzzle (riddle) are being submitted for consideration. The story of God and his people summarized in Psalm 78 has come into its final chapter. What used to be obscure and incomplete, waiting for resolution, has finally found its fullest expression in Jesus' parables of the kingdom. This is how Matthew invests the word "to fulfill" (Matt 13:35) with a powerful and sweeping eschatological tenor. But this aspect of fulfillment also brings in its trail the third tier of truth communicated in the explanatory interlude of 13:34–35, namely, the retelling of the whole story of redemption.

"Master of Suspense" Alfred Hitchcock directed over fifty feature films in his illustrious career as a director, a good number of them belonging to the mystery genre. Most of them do not have the audience in doubt about the villain or the hero, yet without any loss in suspense. If the content of Jesus' kingdom parables had been like a Hitchcock movie in this respect, in other words, if they projected things that everyone could see coming, because Jesus' stories largely aligned with the people's messianic expectations, everything would be different. But the Jesus of history and of the Bible cannot be contained, and his stories solicited more than a lingering uneasiness in the hearers, leaving them wondering, "What might this mean?" As we have argued so far, the parables of the kingdom were plotting a coming of God's reign that no one saw coming, and as a result, many were not only disappointed but offended. The parables, and more generally the Gospel records as presented in the New Testament, require a redefinition of the entire metanarrative of the Old Testament. As Jesus himself taught his disciples (cf. Luke 24:27), all of Scripture, all of redemptive history, is now seen as centered in his person and must be read through the lens of a Christ-centered hermeneutic. But since the story is anchored in him in a way that no one foresaw, God's Old Testament revelation is also retold, as previous Scriptures are seen in the new light that Christ is.

One can only imagine how his disciples were reeling with the import of some of his parables of the kingdom, as they called for a ponderous re-evaluation of much of their inherited sacred writings in terms of Christ's advent and its meaning and implications. It is true that the world has never been the same since Christ, and this also extends to how the Old Testament must be read and understood. For Jesus' contemporaries, the parables as the unveiling of God's reign in the last days signified nothing less than a wholescale revolution of their faith. That this transformation was accomplished in a single generation without breaking their faith is truly remarkable, something that the Lord has done.

Just as the book of Acts shows, it was not only canonical revelation that was consummated and reconstructed in the light of Jesus' ministry. His teachings, including his parables, also forced a redefinition of the people of God, a subversive concept that the apostles and the first-century church needed some time to digest (cf. Acts 10:1–11:18). The parable of the sower only hinted at the radical change of direction from a people defined by national identity to a people solely defined by spiritual prerequisites along the lines fleshed out in Romans 2:25–29. The parables, with their material content, are radical on more than one level. Unlike the surprising ending to a long story of multiple chapters, this final installment changes everything, while still giving ultimate meaning and beautiful cohesion to the entire story from its inception to the end.

Finally, the great challenge of the bird's-eye view that the stories of the kingdom afford remains with us to this day. For if they called for a rethinking of religious convictions among Jewish

The Kingdom Revealed in Its Full Expression

followers of the first century, they certainly stand in conflict with current worldviews and values. The parables require not only a Christ-centered perspective of Old Testament history, but of history *per se*. Nothing remains the same since Christ, and not even our cancel culture with its ahistorical agenda can change this. We must be careful how we make sense of our lives and the time in which we are living. As the world is under the sway of the media that manipulate the public to inculcate the so-called "woke"-driven values, idols, hatred, and fears, as seen recently in the global COVID-19 crisis and social justice slogans, many ask the question, "What is happening, where will this lead, how will this change my life, family, career, plans?" How we think and react to the events that shape our time depends on the story in which we live. If we inhabit Jesus' stories, and indeed his metanarrative, the parables buttress a worldview that does not shift with the passage of time but incorporates all eventualities. The kingdom of God still requires a faith decision, is God's decision, admits of opposition, and continues to succeed through all difficulties, no matter its small beginnings or unobtrusive, hidden growth in the world. Jesus' stories are fixed like the stars and are not subject to reinterpretation or cancellation, because they are not from here. They have come to us from the Father, as his Son professed, and he "makes known to us the mystery of his will, according to his purpose, which he set forth in Christ as a plan for the fullness of time. To unite all things in him, things in heaven and things on earth" (Eph 1:9–10).

"And in Antioch the disciples were first called Christians" (Acts 11:26). Originally, as William Barclay explains in his commentary on Acts 11:26,[8] the word "Christian" was more like a nickname, as the Antiochenes were famous for coming up with all kinds of nicknames. When the bearded Caesar Julian visited the city, they called him "billygoat." The ending *-iani* (as in *Christiani*) was used to signify the notion of belonging to a certain party, the "Christ-people." Though at first, the byname had a contemptuous nuance, Christians made it into one that the whole world couldn't and will never forget. With their lives they showed that it was no

---

8. Barclay, *The Acts of the Apostles*, 105.

contemptible name, but a name that spoke of courage and love. What is it to us today? It remains a challenge, not a badge, but a challenge to continue to trust in Jesus and to have influence with his gospel until the end.

7

The Kingdom's Inestimable Value

WITH THE TWIN PARABLES of the hidden treasure and the pearl we move into the second set of Matthew's collection. The first three likenesses afforded summary views of the kingdom with sweeping panoramas. But in the remaining triple of stories,[1] the focus is squarely on personal experience, namely the joy of receiving the kingdom and the pain of losing everything in the end. Matthew is a master of literary structure, and his sense of symmetry is built into the arrangement of the last three stories, too. They are framed by references to dismal "weeping and gnashing of teeth" (Matt 13: 42, 50), whereas exuberant joy is present at the center of the chiastic structure (13:44), reflecting on the division of two kinds of people that the word of the kingdom produces. In addition to the shift from abstract contemplations to people's subjective experiences, the second half of the chapter also reverses the narrowing trajectory of the first half, thus creating a mirroring effect. While the parables of the sower, the weeds, and the mustard seed move from the many to singularity (one seed/plant) in a funneling motion, the hidden treasure, the pearl, and the dragnet proceed from

---

1. As we have already noted, the fourth parable of the leaven is the connective tissue or hinge between the two parts of the complex.

singularity to the many "fish of every kind" (13:47). So the table is set for the last three parables.

Stallard identifies the man who finds the field as well as the merchant in search for the pearl as pictures of Christ himself. He (ironically) does not consider it a "stretch"[2] to see the hiding of the treasure as Christ's temporary rejection of Israel and the buying of the field as his call to the gentile world, believing that "he has a heart for the world (the field) in light of the treasure itself."[3] But the field is purchased *only* for the sake of the treasure in it! The scenario is not unlike that of Proverbs 2:4, describing the search for wisdom: "If you seek it like silver and search for it as for hidden treasures . . ." The point is the treasure, and the same is true for the parable of the hidden treasure. The field is bought not because the lucky man has a heart for it, but because he is fixed on securing the treasure. The merchant in search of the pearl as a portrait of Christ has more to commend it than the man who finds the treasure by getting lucky. "The Son of Man came to seek and to save the lost" (Luke 19:10), but at no time did he stumble across his treasure. But since the two parables obviously form a unit, their interpretation requires a more integrated approach that can account for not only the similarities, but also the differences. This cannot be done satisfactorily, if Christ identifies with both figures, one being a man on a purposeful quest, the other a lucky duck.

A number of dispensational theologians have pursued a different line of interpretation. Trench identifies the treasure as the Gentiles and the pearl as believing Jews, arguing that the Jews were looking for the coming kingdom, whereas the Gentiles were not.[4] Walvoord reverses the order and argues that the treasure is a symbol of Israel, whose value is unrecognized by the world

---

2. Stallard, "Hermeneutics and Matthew 13," 354.
3. Stallard, "Hermeneutics and Matthew 13," 354.
4. Trench, *Notes on the Parables*, 112–13. In this case, however, one would expect the Jews (pearl) to come first, not the Gentiles. As it is, the parables do not speak of historical redemptive processes, but of personal experience in finding the kingdom.

The Kingdom's Inestimable Value

(field).[5] Yet, locating redemptive historical processes in the twin parables is ill-conceived on several grounds, not the least being the abovementioned focus on personal, subjective experiences. They are introduced for a reason, and it is not to confuse or jumble them with the course of redemptive history.

A few additional contextual considerations are in order. First, the hiddenness of the treasure in its immediate setting is best correlated with Jesus' instruction about teaching in kingdom parables (Matt 13:11–17). For most, the treasure of the kingdom remains hidden, because they "do not see" (13:13). If there are any underlying historical nuances, they can only be found in the mystery of the kingdom that is now revealed in Christ. As he says in 13:17, "For truly, I say to you, many prophets and righteous people longed to see what you see, and did not see it." Again, this notion would harmonize well with Matthew's commentary in 13:35, anchored in the quotation of Psalm 78:2. The mystery of the kingdom had been hidden (like the treasure) "since the foundation of the world." The reference is not to Israel failing to be rightly valued, but to the true nature of the kingdom that is now beginning to be unveiled in Jesus' parables and ministry.

Second, the hidden treasure also relates to the previous set of parables, emphasizing the hidden and unpretentious nature of the kingdom (mustard seed, leaven). This link points to a more inclusive referent than merely Israel. Jesus' concern is with no less than the totality of the kingdom. National distinctions are not in the purview of the story.

Third, the image of the treasure must also be considered in light of Jesus' concluding statement of Matthew 13:52, which is intended as an echo of the parable of the hidden treasure. Accordingly, the treasure of the kingdom belongs to the disciple as his *personal* possession (cf. "who brings out of *his* treasure what is new and what is old," 13:52). This does not chime with an identification of the treasure as national Israel or any related historical processes. Rather, the idea is remarkably parallel to what Jesus teaches in

---

5. Cf. Walvoord, *Matthew*, 104–05. See also Fenton, "The Parables of the Treasure," 178–79.

12:35, looking forward to 13:52: "The good person out of his good treasure brings forth good." The treasure here is identified with "words" (12:37), and the words must be related to the word about the kingdom. In any case, the hidden treasure stresses personal, subjective experience, just as Jesus links the laying up of heavenly treasure in 6:19–21 with the disciple's heart: "For where your treasure is, there your heart will be also." The concept of finding treasure in heaven resurfaces for one last time in Jesus' reply to the rich young man (19:21), who is to sell all his wealth in order to secure the true and lasting riches as his personal possession. So, the twin parables of treasure and pearl operate on the level of subjective experience and add an important nuance to the complex of seven stories.[6]

In late November of 1992, Peter Whatling, a tenant farmer of Suffolk, England, lost a hammer in the fields of his farm. After an unsuccessful search, he asked his friend, Eric Lawes, who owned a metal detector, for help. Lawes's machine buzzed over a particular portion of land when they found a silver spoon that looked quite old. They dug a little deeper and with R-rated exclamations of incredulity uncovered ancient pieces of jewelry along with antique coins. After a complete excavation which unearthed no fewer than fifteen thousand coins, the find turned out to be a fabulous cache of treasure from the late Roman / early Byzantine era (early fifth century AD). The assessed value of the treasure that became known as the "Hoxne Hoard" amounted to about 1.75 million pounds ($3.5 million), in today's currency considerably more.[7]

How many people scour about their property with metal detectors? And even if some would make a hobby of it for lack of better ideas, what is the likelihood of stumbling over a hidden treasure? No one in his right mind would ever bet on such an extreme oddity in the course of life. But we all face decisions about what we value most in life, and this moves us in the direction of

---

6. It may be pointed out that Matthew 7:6 refers to one's personal identification with the kingdom as the possession of "pearls." "Do not throw your pearls before pigs . . ."

7. Mingren, "The Hoxne Hoard."

The Kingdom's Inestimable Value

our twin parables. The valuation of things is determined to a great extent by the factor of time. If something is not enduring or permanent, then how valuable is it? Wealth, riches, and property we can't take with us, as the saying goes. Whatever fortune we may have becomes worthless to us on the day of death.

But, as church father Augustine once said, "He who seeks God finds joy"; the fortune of finding the kingdom of heaven is not limited by time or our own mortality. Jesus said, "Do not lay up for yourselves treasures on earth, where moth and rust destroy and where thieves break in and steal; but lay up for yourselves treasures in heaven, where neither moth nor rust destroys and where thieves do not break in and steal. For where your treasure is, there your heart will be also" (Matt 6:19–21). Likewise, the writer of the letter to the Hebrews affirmed for his addressees that "you knew that yourselves had a better possession and an abiding one" (Heb 10:34). True value resides only in what outlasts a lifetime and remains forever. And here we are squarely within the center of gravity of the two parables of the kingdom's inestimable value. They are closely related, in that their core theme revolves around finding and appreciating ultimate value. In fact, they are parallel in no fewer than five ways, each featuring a reference to something of great value, the event of finding, going, selling, and eventually buying the valued object.[8] But the parable of the hidden treasure also differs from the pearl in terms of the *manner* of finding.

The man who finds a treasure in the field can only be described as a "lucky bastard" (German: "Glückspilz"). He is not combing the landscape with a metal detector, but simply gets lucky in a most extravagant way, as he stumbles across a treasure. The background of the image is of a known practice in first-century Palestinian culture. The tenuous times of the first century AD leading up to the Jewish War of 66–70 certainly produced numbers of roaming brigands and rapacious Roman soldiers, and in the absence of banks to deposit wealth, burying treasure in the ground was the preferred way to ensure its safety.[9]

---

8. Cf. Stallard, "Hermeneutics and Matthew 13," 354.
9. Hill, *The Gospel of Matthew*, 238.

Old and New

The merchant and the pearl of great value, however, is a different case. With his expert eyes on the market, the travelling merchant has been scouring the agoras and plazas far and wide for the deal of a lifetime, the pearl of all pearls, and finding it spells the end of his search. I believe the two stories elucidate the same reality from different angles. On the one hand, the kingdom of heaven is like the treasure. Jesus Christ and the salvation he offers come to the finder without effort or merit, as a free gift, so to speak. The idea is reflected in Jesus' words to his disciples: "To you it has been given to know the secrets of the kingdom of heaven" (Matt 13:11), "blessed are your eyes, for they see" (13:16).

Then again, although the kingdom is received as a divine gift, it still wants to be sought above all else, as Jesus affirmed, "Seek first the kingdom of God and his righteousness" (Matt 6:33). In this sense, the parable of the pearl acts like a counterbalance to Jesus' teaching of the kingdom as a free gift from the Father in heaven. As we have noted, the kingdom requires a decision on our part, although it is also a decision that God has already made for us. As for the former notion, the rich young man of 19:16–22 is a perfect foil for the expert merchant. He earnestly seeks eternal life, but is not prepared to sell all that he has to obtain heavenly treasure, which is precisely the transaction portrayed in the parable.[10] Selling all that one has rests on a value judgment, a rating of priorities, and for the one who finds Christ, he becomes the pearl of ultimate value that warrants a radical and joyful response. In the end, it makes no difference whether one finds life in Christ as the lucky fellow or as one who has always been searching for the meaning of life and purpose, for in both cases, the response is the same and remain so throughout the life of a follower of Christ. For even the lucky finder, after his amazing discovery, sells all his belongings to secure the field. In other words, he goes for broke and recklessly stakes everything on one card to retain the treasure. The chains of actions that lead to taking possession of the treasure and purchasing the pearl both point to the value seen in the object. The emphasis of the twin stories is on an initial total reorientation of

---

10. Note Jesus' words in 19:21, "and you will have treasure in heaven..."

The Kingdom's Inestimable Value

priorities when the kingdom of God is encountered. But the paradigm shift of value also has inceptive implications and does not only concern those who come to Christ for the first time in their lives. After all, the preciousness of the heavenly gift is timeless, but our valuation of it isn't. So, in the course of our lifetime, we have need of being reminded of our true treasure in heaven versus the material things in front of us, in order to reconfirm and settle for our initial valuation of the kingdom of heaven.

The famous siege of Weinsberg in the modern state of Baden-Württemberg, Germany, illustrates the point in a vivid way. Around the year 1140, the struggle between two dynasties, the Welfs and the Hohenstaufen, came to a head. Emperor Conrad III of the house of Hohenstaufen laid siege to Weinsberg under Count Welf to bring it and him under his rule. The distress of the men, women, and children shut in the city was extreme, and they sought refuge in the count's castle. Eventually, the fortress was breached, too, but the emperor wanted to show himself chivalrous and granted the women and children safe withdrawal before the castle's capitulation. He also granted them anything that they could carry in their own strength, while the men were to be prisoners of war. What did they take? Food? Possessions? They carried their husbands on their backs and headed out of town, past the baffled soldiers. Conrad had the dignity to honor his word and ordered his troops to stand down and let them pass. The clever and loyal wives bore their treasure out of Weinsberg.[11]

The emphasis of the two parables of the treasure and the pearl lies in what they have in common. Both the lucky man and the merchant, upon recognizing what they have found, joyfully sell all that they have to buy the one object of their desire. Both invest in the kingdom with all their heart and soul because they consider the value of what they have.[12] The parables do not suggest that one

---

11. Køppen, *The World in the Middle Ages*, 131–32.

12. The re-hiding in the case of the treasure has been interpreted variously. But it seems best to view the act as a direct result of the joy of finding it ("on account of his joy," Matt 13:44). The re-hiding is thus the first of three steps that lead to the securing of the treasure, moving from the re-hiding to the selling of all his possessions to the purchase of the field. All three are governed by

could pay for a berth in the kingdom, no more than one could purchase salvation. The great price of our redemption has been paid by our Lord Jesus Christ, who is our treasure. He emptied himself of his glory, came to earth in the form of a servant, and offered up his blood on the cross to pay the divine penalty for our sins and to secure redemption. Jesus' sacrifice opens the gates to God's kingdom, but when he reveals himself to our hearts to make us see him as the great treasure of his kingdom, everything changes. When "the eyes of our hearts" (Eph 1:18) are enlightened, the value system of the world is turned on its head, as Jesus taught, "what is exalted among men is an abomination in the sight of God" (Luke 16:15). The most important things are not seen with the naked eye, but with the heart.[13] The kingdom of heaven is the real treasure and pearl of great value because it is lasting. All earthly treasure is fleeting. Ancient kings had their extreme wealth buried with them, but where are they now? All earthly possessions cease to be ours (if they ever were!) when we die. But if we find the kingdom as our enduring treasure in Christ, no one can rob our joy, for it ultimately rests in God's hands from where it came to us.

With the dominant theme of finding and joyfully selling all, the twin parables add psychological depth to the collection of Matthew 13.[14] They elucidate the "bliss" that Jesus introduced as "seeing" and "hearing" the mysteries of the kingdom in Matthew 13:11–12 from a personal, subjective perspective, an element that was largely absent from the previous parables of the kingdom. Finding and *seeing* the treasure of the kingdom and the value of the pearl does something to you. The lucky fellow's life is forever changed, as he will never again have to worry about eking out a

---

the joy and anticipation of the lucky man. As Bailey shows, finding a treasure without any mark of ownership (which appears to be assumed in the parable) in order to acquire it was considered legal in rabbinic traditions. Cf. Bailey, "The Parables of the Hidden Treasure and of the Pearl Merchant," 180.

13. Cf. de Saint Exupéry, *The Little Prince*.

14. This is true for all the parables up to this point with the exception of the parable of the sower. Its emphasis on the hearer's decision to either heed or reject the message of the kingdom also features a subjective focus.

The Kingdom's Inestimable Value

living, and the merchant's tenacious search for the elusive pearl has ended. After the deal of a lifetime he will retire.

Where do I belong? What is the purpose of my life? How much is enough?—All these questions are put to bed once we have found Christ as our treasure and keep him in front of us, along with the incorruptible inheritance through God's love in him, and further searching becomes unnecessary. Jesus Christ meets all our needs, satisfies our longings, heals us and makes us whole before God our Father. He also gives us hope for the future, no matter our present circumstances, for he says, "Fear not, little flock, for it is your Father's good pleasure to give you the kingdom" (Luke 12:32). Is it your treasure? Then what are you willing to give for it? We say, "Beauty is in the eye of the beholder." If the beauty and inherent value of the kingdom is seen with the heart, no sacrifice is too great to make for such a treasure.[15] It will always remain the bargain of a lifetime.

Paul says, "One thing I do: forgetting what lies behind and straining forward to what lies ahead" (Phil 3:13). Enduring in the here and now is hard when we feel that God's promises are fulfilled in other people's lives, but not in ours. Often, we yearn for the good old times in the past. But we ought to always look ahead to the great reward, for the joy of the kingdom is ours and still to be obtained in fullness. We want to mobilize our focus and strength and look to the finish line like a competitor. The prize justifies our devotion, for God has called us to eternal life. So each day carries a new dimension. We can live it in plain sight of the kingdom of heaven.

The extreme runner Rafael Fuchsgruber has run through the deserts of this world, including some 520 kilometers in nine days through the Australian outback. He wrote the names of his wife and daughter on the tips of his running shoes, so that they were always before him, step by step. He explained the habit by referring to how important it is in crisis to keep one's focus in order to persevere and not to throw in the towel. He looked at the names on his shoes and imagined how he would come home to his loved ones

---

15. Cf. Sider, "Interpreting the Hid Treasure," 371.

to embrace them and to have a great time with them after the run. Each time he did, he was strengthened in his resolve. The hope that inspires us and gives us wings in the midst of here and now and at the end of our journey of life is Christ's kingdom of heaven. It is our treasure and pearl now and will be our possession to the full measure in the consummation.

8

The Kingdom Asserts Universal Claim

A CREW OF SEINE fishers lower their dragnet. Its bottom edge held down by weights and its top edge buoyed by floats, the net hangs vertically in the deep and traps whatever swims in its path. The mariners know exactly what they are looking for, tuna, swordfish, or some other kind, but the coveted creatures will come up with a host of other things, including trash. Sorting out the catch is part and parcel of the trade. Jesus' parable of the dragnet draws on a time-honored fishing technique. Some of his own disciples like Peter and John belonged to a guild of men who fished the Sea of Galilee[1] in such manner for sardines or tilapia, which almost certainly yielded the inspiration for the analogy.

The parable is the seventh of its kind in chapter 13 and brings the collection of stories to a splendid close. Its individual features provide links with all the previous parables at both thematic and lexical levels and thus firmly ground the integrity of the entire discourse. Our discussion begins with a brief synopsis of the textual links.

---

1. Also known as the Lake of Tiberias.

The dragnet certainly harks back to the parable of the sower.[2] The two stories frame the complex of Matthew 13 and deliver snapshots of both the beginning and the end. The kingdom, contrary to common expectations, begins with the sowing of the word in Jesus' own teaching ministry and carried on through his disciples, but its power will not be on full display until judgment day, "the close of the age" (Matt 13:49) depicted in the dragnet. The framing stories also feature thematic elements that interact with each other in interesting ways. Both the sowing of seed in every place and the gathering of fish of every kind share a certain indiscrimination, yet with opposite thrusts. The seed is tossed *out* while the fish is dragged *in*. Like the opening and the closing of a fist, the idea is of a centrifugal (outward), then centripetal (inward) force. The kingdom has universal appeal and asserts universal claim over people. The call is to all, and in the end, irrespective of the various responses, no one can escape its assertion of power and ownership.

The parable of the dragnet also has unmistakable, strong links with the parable of the weeds. Both are characterized by an uncompromising dichotomy of good and evil and by their final separation. The apocalyptic depiction of judgment day as involving ministering angels, a "fiery furnace," and the "weeping and gnashing of teeth" (13:42, 50) in both cases creates an audible, almost refrain-like effect for emphasis. Unlike the weeds, however, the dragnet offers no hint at any struggle between the good and the evil, as its (nearly) exclusive focal point is the end of the age.

The twin parables of the mustard seed and the leaven accentuate the *ex*tensive and *in*tensive growth of the kingdom. They have no concern with the judgment, but their common trajectory towards fullness surely connects with the dragnet. "When it was grown" (ὅταν δὲ αὐξηθῇ, 13:32), "until it was leavened" (ἕως οὗ ἐζυμώθη, 13:33), and "when it was full" (ὅτε ἐπληρώθη, 13:48) are three very similar constructs involving conjunctions (in the case of ἕως, 13:33, a preposition), followed by passive aorists, and all three have a consistent stress on the fullness of time. It is only in the fullness of time that God's reign is fully realized—for good and for ill.

---

2. See the details in the first chapter of this work.

The Kingdom Asserts Universal Claim

As for the hidden treasure and the pearl, their unique theme of finding and selling portrays a radical value judgment in favor of the kingdom. Its worth exceeds all other possessions and more than justifies the sacrifice of all. An assessment of value is integral to both and is the joint between the twin parables and the dragnet. The last three parables involve a rigorous value judgment in which only the good is retained. Everything else is either thrown away (13:50) or given up and relinquished. So, the "sons of the kingdom" (13:38) acquire the kingdom by selling all they have, and the Son of Man's angels collect the good by separating them from the bad.

At the same time, the dragnet completes the picture of the two preceding parables. In the latter, all is happily sacrificed to obtain the kingdom, while the dragnet emphasizes what will happen if this transaction does not occur. The ominous warning is already declared in 13:12, that whatever perishable good one thinks to have and clings to in this life will be taken away. All that remains is incessant weeping and gnashing of teeth in the outer place of gloom, a total loss. The contrasting themes of loss and gain are also couched in a chiastic structure. Weeping and gnashing of teeth (13:42, 50) on account of total loss contain the joy of gaining the ultimate treasure in the field (13:44).[3] The same arrangement points to another common denominator of the second table of parables, as the dragnet continues to accentuate subjective experience *vis-à-vis* the eschatological trajectory of the kingdom of God.[4] Exuberant joy and bottomless despair run the gamut of human emotions and bring balance to the entire complex of seven, inasmuch as the first half of the chapter features no emotional responses.

The parable of the dragnet, with its apocalyptic horizon, once again underscores that Jesus thought of himself as the Son of Man of Daniel 7, to whom is given the judgment of the nations. His power and authority to execute the final sentence comes from the Ancient of Days (Dan 7:13-14; cf. John 5:22). His dominion is universal, and all nations must give account to him. The idea of

---

3. Joy is certainly also implied in the pearl, though not explicit.
4. The same point is made by Donahue, *The Gospel in Parable*, 69.

the Day of the Lord is firmly anchored in the Old Testament, as is the final separation of good and evil. But, as the parable also makes clear, evil will not be removed from the world until the close of the age. The interim period of sowing the word with all its ambiguity and the delay of his glorious reign for all eternity introduce a tension that few, if any, of Jesus' contemporaries would have contemplated or even allowed for.

This holdup or gap, of course, solicits the question as to whether the gathering of the fish is meant to portray the evangelization of the nations in the inter-advent period. Hagner suggests that it "may be an intentional reflection of the universality of the invitation to accept the good news of the kingdom."[5] The universal call of the gospel is certainly implied in the first phase of the venture,[6] the catching of every kind of creature. Two reasons force this conclusion. First, the immediate context of Matthew 13, in particular the parable of the sower of the word, must be allowed to shape our understanding of the dragnet. The sharing of the good news is one of the hallmarks of the unexpected coming of the kingdom in this age, and it cannot be eliminated from consideration. Second, the trade of fishing has already been put to service in Matthew as an analogy of the disciples' evangelizing efforts. Jesus called them to be "fishers of men" (cf. Matt 4:19). The idea lies just beneath the surface of the dragnet.

All this being said, evangelization is only a peripheral concern of this parable, far from being the primary stress.[7] Bailey claims that "the gospel must be preached to all classes of people because God is 'not willing that any should perish'" (2 Pet 3:9).[8] This is true, but requires a good deal of imagination to obtain from the brief story. By the same token, the mixture of good and bad inside the net is hardly a call for the church to patient waiting. The point has already been made in the tale of the weeds, which explains

---

5. Hagner, *Matthew 1–13*, 399.

6. See also, Bailey, "The Parables of the Dragnet and of the Householder," 284–85.

7. Cf. Dodd, *The Parables of the Kingdom*, 151.

8. Bailey, "The Parables of the Dragnet and of the Householder," 290.

The Kingdom Asserts Universal Claim

the origin of conflict about the kingdom, but patience as a virtue is at best *implicit* here, as there is no hint whatsoever of conflict. The gathering of the fish is a necessary feature of the parable, but clearly subservient to what follows, the sorting out of the catch.

Therefore, the center of gravity is found in three related ideas. First, the story's stress is on the separation of good and bad, a separation that has already begun in how people respond to the kingdom's word (sower), but will be final and eternal on the same ground (response) at the end of the age. This is where the sole focus of Jesus' commentary lies (Matt 13:49–50), which is an indication of how he wanted the parable to be rendered. Hand in hand with the final separation is the value judgment upon which it rests. The distinction of two kinds was key to the weeds, and it remains the question looming over the dragnet, along with the above personal questions posed by it.

But the third and perhaps dominant idea, which readers often fail to recognize, is the universal sway that the kingdom holds over all humans. The notion is so obvious that it is too easy to ignore or overlook: the kingdom asserts universal claim. Although the kingdom flies under the radar of the world's attention and its message remains the most underrated of all messages, everyone will eventually have to answer to the King and face the reality of his sovereign power. In one way or another, we are already caught in the net, and every human's destiny is inevitably entangled in the grand story of the kingdom that determines the shape of world history. Each one will be found to play a role in the epic drama in the end, for good or for ill, irrespective of our awareness of it at this time. The dragnet is cast and the process underway, putting everyone on a collision course with the universal ultimatum of the kingdom.

It is therefore clear that the last of the seven stories raises the question of identity and ultimately of belonging. As we indicated earlier, the dragnet comes with an emotional appeal to abysmal suffering and pain. Its warning forces some searching personal inquiries. When the net is pulled up, what will be my experience? Will I be found to be good or bad? Judgment will be on the basis of how one responds to the message of the kingdom, and the positive, right response is depicted in the joy that governs the chain of actions in the hidden treasure and the pearl. So, the specter of our eternal destiny, with the looming threat of eternal damnation, is raised again and with even greater intensity than in the parable of the weeds. Jesus knew that our life on earth is short and only a prelude to eternity. As such, it must decide over where and how we will be. If we live with our focus on earth, even what we have will be lost forever (13:12). But if Jesus is our treasure and delight, and if we live God-ward, the kingdom is ours and our experience will be like dinner: the best comes at last. Total loss or total gain is the motto. How then would our life goals change if we planned not only for this life but eternity? "For where your treasure is, there your heart will be also" (Matt 6:21).

About fifty years ago, there was a great spiritual awakening on the Indonesian island of Timor. It was triggered by a famous marathon runner who relied on his amulet for winning competitions. One night, as he lay in bed, he turned numb and his body was paralyzed. He cried to God and promised that he would get rid of his lucky charm. The paralysis passed subsequently. So he went to his pastor and gave him his amulet. On the following Sunday, the runner gave his testimony in the worship service. Suddenly, not the least because the man was a public figure, congregants began to pray, and some confessed their own sins of sorcery, while others went home to fetch their lucky charms and talismans, as well as other items of dark magic. All of them were burned in a bonfire in front of the church building, and the congregation experienced an overwhelming outpouring of the Holy Spirit. How big would such a heap be if we all got rid of our own charms that compete with our Lord, whatever things we may cling to for delivering happiness, security, and success? How joyful many would be in the freedom of the faith!

Then again, we are like a patient in a hospital bed, staring at the walls. We are held back and tied down by a host of things, our weakness, sin, and mortality. We keep looking at a calendar on one wall, wondering what we should do or what we may miss. A cross

The Kingdom Asserts Universal Claim

hangs on the other wall. Our eyes constantly move from one wall to the opposite, between calendar and cross. The calendar speaks of important things beyond count that need to get done and vie for our attention. But on the other side the little cross speaks a different language in the sound of silence. "I have suffered for you, I died for you. Look to me." In one way or another, our choice is one of two, as there are only two ways to live in this world. And even now, we are somehow caught in the net, for Jesus' parable reduces the passage of time and every human life to a single fishing venture that catches only two kinds, the good and the bad. That makes me one of the two.

The parables' cardinal teaching, the kingdom's universal sway over all, is also a perfect follow-up to the closely related story of the weeds, with its apocalyptic flavor. The latter's function was—in part—to account for the opposition against Jesus that led up to Matthew 13 and the world's continuing opposition right up until the end of time. Matthew's arrangement of the parables already hinted at the sovereign purpose of God in allowing his enemies to stick to their guns and (seemingly) sabotage the kingdom's advance throughout time.[9] But in the dragnet, we see no trace of opposition, only one seamless venture that moves towards its inevitable conclusion. The sovereign power of the kingdom determines the shape of all things, from beginning to end, and therefore even opposition must serve its overall purpose. And indeed, what better way to demonstrate total sway than to admit of opposition in order to display absolute, unmitigated authority over all! The King's sovereignty is heightened by the circumstances and environment which he rules. The catch of fish is brought to shore and sorted out, and nothing gets away from the dragnet's mesh. The entire enterprise is God's sovereign action; no race or category will escape the final judgment and the full realization of the kingdom.[10] "For from him and through him and to him are all things. To him be glory forever" (Rom 11:36).

---

9. See the discussion in chapter 3.
10. Cf. Blomberg, *Interpreting the Parables*, 202.

9

Old and New in Perspective

"No one, after drinking old wine, desires new, for he says, 'The old is good'" (Luke 5:39). Jesus knew full well that his teachings were new in some sense, indeed, too new for his bitter opponents. Things are not necessarily good because they are old, nor are things bad because they are new. But their own time-honored doctrines and tradition were more palatable to the scribes and Pharisees, while they fancied Jesus' teaching not only as novel but downright dangerous and subversive to their religious culture. Their reluctance to even consider something that they judged as new was ironic, because even Jesus' "new things" were more ancient than theirs. The turn that the New Testament takes with Jesus at the helm was in reality only consistent with God's plans from of old, even if few could see it at the time. New and old, therefore, is a nomenclature in need of some explanation before it can be rightly understood. On the other hand, Matthew 13:52 affirms that Jesus' teaching did indeed involve bringing out of one's "treasure what is new and what is old."

One must not overlook that the saying of 13:52 itself declares a new guild of custodians of God's treasure of revelation—Jesus'

Old and New in Perspective

disciples. So this is more than just a "happy postscript,"[1] but Jesus' followers are knighted as the new scribes of the kingdom.[2] New things call for new householders, new representatives, new scribes (a term that generally comes freighted with negative connotations in the Gospels, but not here). Jesus entrusts his church with the rich deposit of revealed truth to make people see and treasure the King and to explain the hidden things of his kingdom.

What is new is in many cases no more than a difference in degree, the clarification of things that the Old Testament already sketches in some vague way. But now, in Jesus' parables, what used to be obscure and ambivalent is taught with clarity and final authority. Of course, the words of Jesus also spell the end of old things. There would never again be a temple made with hands, no more sacrifices, and no Israel of God defined in terms of ethnicity. New, however, does not mean complicated in the sense that older people are sometimes afraid to embrace new technology because this would call for learning the unfamiliar. As the parable of the sower indicates, the scenario is most simple: The call of the kingdom to repent and believe in the Son of God goes out, and whoever believes is in. The parables of Jesus always demand a decision in favor of God, whose love is manifest in sending his Son for the salvation of the lost. There are no prerequisites, no rituals or initiations required, only faith in the word. The situation would be like a little Berlin boy who asks a fine lady how to get to Kurfürstendamm. The noble lady musters the boy from head to toe and says, "Boy, if you want something from me, you must first pull your hands out of your pockets, take off your hat, wipe your nose, and address me with 'Madam' while you make a bow." But the boy replies, "No thanks, that's all too much for me. Then I'd rather get lost!" New is not complicated but simple and open, and the offer of God's love and forgiveness is as liberal as sunshine.

On the other hand, the kingdom call is radical and spells total surrender. The problem that Jesus' contemporaries had with his doctrine was, after all, not its newness *per se*, but the change that it

---

1. Morris, *The Gospel According to Matthew*, 362.
2. Cf. Bailey, "The Parables of the Dragnet and the Householder," 291-92.

required. The parables demand a decision, and this decision is tied to the person of Jesus Christ, who referred to himself as the Son of Man. So one fine day, you think that you are okay, but then comes Jesus and says, "The time is fulfilled, the kingdom of God is near, repent and believe in the gospel!" (Mark 1:15). Their real problem (as is ours) is perhaps captured in the ironic words of a pastor to a young man. The young man says, "Pray with me that I may be able to find my way out of bed earlier in the morning!" "Gladly," says the pastor. "When you pull one foot out of your bed, I will pray for you that you may also be able to pull out the other." When it comes to Christ's claims and the call to bear our cross after him, we tend to make lame excuses, or seek to try on different crosses for a better personal fit. It was the same two thousand years ago. The gospel of the crucified Christ will always force a choice, as much as God's grace works in us both to will and to do of his good pleasure (Phil 2:13).

But what did Jesus think of the kingdom of heaven based on his famous parables? What does he mean by "what is new"? It is clear that Matthew placed the discourse of seven parables of the kingdom at the center of his account of Jesus' life and that he thought of this collection as representative of Christ's unique teaching style. Parables as a didactic device were not at all unheard of in first-century Judaism, but Jesus' stories were almost invariably about the kingdom of heaven, and this was a novelty. Irrespective of the distinct cultural and religious environment of his time, we can certainly say that Jesus' parables constitute a very unique departure from established biblical instruction. Perhaps their closest match is found in the proverbial wisdom literature of the Old Testament and very few prophetic parables like Isaiah 5:1–7. On the whole, though, the parables, with their unique focus on the kingdom, are exceptional and lack any equivalent in Scripture.[3]

The first question to raise, therefore, would be how the cluster of parables in Matthew 13 functions in the Gospel as a whole, as

---

3. This is true for both Old Testament and New Testament. The Jesus of the Synoptic Gospels used parables profusely, but this cannot be said of the remaining New Testament documents.

Old and New in Perspective

well as the entire New Testament canon. As for the former, the collection near the center of Matthew's account forms the bridge between the two longest teaching discourses in the Gospel, the so-called Sermon on the Mount (5:1—7:27) and the Olivet Discourse (24:3—25:46). In a real sense, the collection of seven parables is right in between them both. The Sermon on the Mount shares with Matthew 13 the prolific use of the expression "kingdom of heaven." But while the Sermon focuses on the ethics of the kingdom, the parables of chapter 13 provide a more sustained theological perspective with a wide-angle lens. They are therefore the theological complement to the Sermon on the Mount. On the other hand, at least two of the parables (weeds, dragnet) feature a narrow eschatological emphasis on the end of the world and judgment day, with their weight clearly more present in the second half of Matthew 13.[4] This means that the parables, with their gradually mounting, topical accent on the end, quite literally "lean" towards the Olivet Discourse, which is even more exclusively preoccupied with the second coming of the Son of Man and the end of time.

With regards to Matthew 13 and the kingdom parables' function in the overall New Testament canon, we may say the following. Not only is the presence of Jesus, the Son of Man, at the beginning and end of the New Testament canon (cf. Rev 1:12–16) literarily pleasing and theologically significant, in that his person and work, as the A and Ω of God's designs, brings closure to the New Testament, but his parables in the Gospels and in particular here in Matthew 13 form the foil or counterpart to his visions in Revelation.[5] Granted, the visionary imagery of the book of Revelation is at times decidedly more grotesque than most of the more pastoral parables of the kingdom of heaven. But the parables share with the visions the heightened use of metaphor, and therefore call

---

4. Jesus' commentary on the parable of the weeds comes with a delay, namely in the second half of the discourse, which lands it in the more immediate neighborhood of the parable of the dragnet towards the conclusion of Matthew 13.

5. As is well known, the book of Revelation is also structured in "sevens," not the least being the three cycles of seven seals, trumpets, and bowls of judgment.

for a special act of translation on the part of the interpreter, as well as the idiosyncratic, panoramic view of ultimate reality that comes with metaphor. It is not only the eschatological thrust of many (or most) of the parables, but their ability to portray complex ideas in a single sweep, similar to the visions in Revelation, that align them with the climax of biblical prophecy in the last book of the Bible. In this way, Jesus' parables as part of the introduction of the New Testament offer a hint or preview of how the book will close, namely with word pictures that, like the stories of Matthew 13, open sweeping vistas of God's plan for the world and his kingdom, sure to come and to prevail. The parables and the visions of the Apocalypse are driven by a simple, common promise: Jesus wins. With this in mind, we can now turn to a summary view of how Jesus' parables offer new perspectives on old truths, or even teach truths that had never been revealed in the first place.

The Kingdom of Heaven in Two Stages

The Old Testament prophetic visions of the last days tend to combine important aspects of the coming of the kingdom without discrimination. Like a landscape viewed without depth or a proper notion of distance, the promises of God appear in a single sweep. So, for example, the inclusion of the Gentiles in God's covenant, the coming of the Davidic king, and the Day of the Lord are all blended together and keep each other's company as the Old Testament expectations of the last days. As a result, they give the appearance of simultaneous fulfillment, or at least fulfillment without much delay. Jesus' parables of the kingdom provide a degree of resolution that was nothing but astonishing for his listeners. There would actually be two comings of the Messiah, and only the second one would usher in the kingdom in power and eternal glory. The present age has seen the inauguration of the kingdom, as Jesus himself affirmed in his earthy ministry (Mark 1:15), but the eschatological distinction introduced in Jesus' parables with respect to the consummation is not for those who cannot wait. Nonetheless, Matthew 13, along with a host of additional stories, prepares the reader for this reality of a kingdom already present but not yet fully realized.

The Kingdom of Heaven as Not of This World

The parables of the kingdom afford greater clarity and authority on the question of eternal destiny, heaven and hell. The only Old Testament text that speaks clearly of an afterlife or the resurrection life beyond this world would be Daniel 12:1-3. It anticipates both a resurrection to glory for the faithful and a resurrection to shame for the rest. Matthew 13:43 alludes to that text. Jesus' parables throw the otherworldliness of the kingdom into relief, along with all practical implications, as, for example, in the parables of the hidden treasure and the pearl. The common notion of the messianic reign involved a kingdom of Israel, even if transformed, but nonetheless along the lines of Old Testament realities under David and Solomon.

The Kingdom of Heaven Reveals Old Things in New Light

Jesus' final words in 13:52 assume a unity of new and old. Both come from the same treasure chest; both, therefore, speak of the kingdom that Jesus came to proclaim. The proper relation of the two is that of promise and fulfillment. The concept includes old forms that shaped the religious life and worship of Israel during Old Testament times. Sacrifices, rituals, the Levitical priesthood, the Jerusalem temple, all these and more belong to an old form that pointed to the new in types and shadows of coming things (cf. Heb 9:6-28). Jesus himself used the antithesis of old and new in this way in Matthew 9:16:

> No one puts a piece of unshrunk cloth on an old garment, for the patch tears away from the garment, and a worse tear is made. Neither is new wine put into old wineskins. If it is, the skins burst and the wine is spilled

and the skins are destroyed. But new wine is put into fresh wineskins, and so both are preserved.

But the antithesis does not suggest wholesale discontinuity. Rather, since the coming of Jesus, old revelation is seen in a new light, as the new revelation is key to a proper and fuller appreciation of the old.[6] Thus, new things do not only signal a new age of the kingdom, but also proffer a new understanding of old things. Everything changes, as everything gains fullness in Christ's teaching.

The Kingdom Requires a Decision

The interim period between the two comings of Christ is a period of the preaching of the word. Faith and not ethnicity decides who belongs to the Israel of God and who does not. In conjunction with the rest of Jesus' teachings, this means that a person's destiny hinges on one's relationship to him whom God has sent, the Son of Man, who will also judge the world. His parables relentlessly press home the point that there is no way around the Son of Man, and the question on Jesus' lips during his final visit to Jerusalem is echoing through the corridors of time: "What do you think about the Christ?" (Matt 22:42).

The Kingdom Is a Free Gift

Here is the flipside of the previous point. While the kingdom demands a faith-based response to the word that is sown in the hearts of every kind of people, the response is not merely generated by human willpower (cf. John 1:12–13). As Jesus makes clear in Matthew 13:11–17, seeing and hearing spiritually is a divine gift, and those who receive it are pronounced "blessed." In the final analysis, therefore, the kingdom is God's decision and must be so in its very nature. Jesus' teaching in Matthew 13 removes the kingdom from the grasp of anyone whom God will not *grant* faith to believe its

---

6. Morris, *The Gospel According to Matthew*, 363.

message. This certainly alienated many of Jesus' contemporaries, who believed that the kingdom belonged to Israel by birthright and old covenant, and only the notorious transgressors had reason to tremble about their participation in God's reign.

The Kingdom Admits of Opposition

A further corollary of the interim period or the already-but-not-yet of the kingdom is that in the present age God's people will continue to suffer and so follow the lead of their Old Testament brothers and sisters and of Jesus Christ himself. The parable of the weeds provides a commanding survey of the epic conflict that goes back to the very beginning. Contrary to Jewish expectation, the coming of the promised Davidic King did not terminate the hostilities between the sons of the kingdom and the sons of the evil one. If anything, Jesus seemed to believe that they will intensify in the last days between his first and especially shortly before his second advent. The idea of the great tribulation Jesus obtained chiefly from Daniel 7—12 (cf. Dan 12:1), although the suffering of God's people is integral to the entire history of redemption since the declaration of war in Genesis 3:15.

The Kingdom Has Small Beginnings

Closely related to the concept of sustained opposition is that of humble beginnings for the messianic age. It is safe to say that nearly all first-century Jews anticipated the coming of the Messiah with a sensational bombshell. But the two parables of growth (mustard seed, leaven), while affirming the unstoppable, yes, even miraculous, expansion of the kingdom, both put a damper on things and have a decidedly inhibiting effect. The kingdom comes with unobtrusive, inconspicuous appeal. As elusive and small as a mustard seed and hidden from the naked eye like yeast in a lump of dough, the kingdom will take everyone by surprise, all the more when its final greatness is revealed. It is certain that Jesus thought of his own ignominious death on the cross as the humble seed from which breathtaking growth would spring.

The Kingdom Comes with Power and Universal Claim

The last point is already included in the first, but it bears repetition. Just as the word is sown in every place, the dragnet of the kingdom will bring to shore every creature without fail. The kingdom will eventually come with power and universal claim. At the final conflagration, when the kingdom comes in its final power and glory, God will at once overrule all opposition, and the human race, irrespective of ethnic origins, will face the ultimate separation of good and evil. This separation has begun in the sowing and hearing of the word, but will be complete at the close of the age. In light of the looming final separation, the human race is referred back to the message of God's great salvation, captured in the parable of the sower. Our eternal destiny rides on our response to and perseverance in the gospel that is now preached to every creature under heaven.

In the end, we can now appreciate how and why the kingdom parables gave Jesus' contemporaries a scare or disappointed them in light of their messianic expectations. However, his stories have lost none of their potency and continue to confront us with their earth-shaking challenges. They are also posing the greatest challenges for us. Nothing much has changed in this regard. The demand for watching and waiting in the present age, the call for perseverance and steadfastness in the light of a host of problems within and without is rife with difficulties, especially if we attempt to walk in our own strength, as we often do. Meanwhile, the global village continues to shrink, and the proliferation of slogans and values that shape the way people think is now delivered with lightning speed. Processes of cultural shifts and opinion formation which used to take decades or centuries and were fairly limited to certain geographic regions now virtually happen overnight and have instant global appeal. The recent COVID-19 crisis, with its global fallout, demonstrated the power of the media megaphone in steering people's and governments' decisions. The total claim of the kingdom of Christ now more than ever sounds like a fading voice from a distant, forgotten world.

Then again, the world's hostility against the message of the kingdom and the Christian church has reached new heights today across the globe and is not likely to abate, but will continue to the end. Too many professing Christians remain opaque at best and submit to the common sentiments of the rule of majority. The parables of the sower and the weeds draw attention to the threat of persecution that has caused and will cause many to take offence and fall away by playing it safe. But in the end, persecution comes not only in the form of outright hostility. The war of two kingdoms is spiritual, and the devil also deploys the lures of the world as portrayed in the sower by the imagery of suffocating thorns. These weapons in disguise do their own to distract and weaken Christians, especially those who live in plain sight of relative affluence and the pleasure-driven culture of the Western hemisphere. The strategy works smoothly, much like a boat taken out by the drift without noticeable friction, but which ends up in open waters without compass, navigation, or orientation, a lost vessel adrift on a vast ocean. Many have sought their fortune in some other worldly venue after having heard and believed the gospel. The call to take stock of the inestimable value of the kingdom over against earthly goods (hidden treasure, pearl) can reach us with considerable muffling in the concert of the competing voice of the ever-changing marketplace of present-day Babylon. Indeed, it can become completely muted.

And finally, living life in the human plane with an eternal perspective in front of us can not only be tiring, but at times seems counterproductive and useless when things need to get done. Who has not been infected by this virus? The image of the man in the hospital bed whose eyes swing like a pendulum from the calendar to the cross may serve as a reminder that the decision to invest in the kingdom of heaven must be renewed every day and remains nonnegotiable. But there is never a good or valid reason to despair. With God all things shall be possible, and his faithfulness ensures the successful passage of all his children through thick and thin, from here to there. As Gustav Heinemann, former president of West Germany, declared in 1950, "Let us answer the world whenever it wants to make us fearful: The lords of your world are going, our Lord is coming."[7] He lays the honor and glory of his own name on the line to raise the stakes for us to take courage in him. He will never give away his glory. When all is said and done, the kingdom and salvation belong to the Lord, and this is our peace even in most difficult times, for he carries us, as "the eternal God is your refuge, and underneath are the everlasting arms" (Deut 33:27). Jesus said, "The one who endures to the end will be saved" (Matt 24:15), but he also vowed that not a single one of his sheep will be lost. "This is the will of him who sent me, that I should lose nothing of all that he has given me, but raise it up on the last day. For this is the will of my Father, that everyone who looks on the Son and believes in him should have eternal life, and I will raise him up on the last day" (John 6:39–40). May his kingdom come!

---

7. Teuffel, "Lasst uns der Welt."

Bibliography

Aitken, Jonathan. *John Newton: From Disgrace to Amazing Grace*. Wheaton, IL: Crossway, 2013.
Bailey, Mark L. "The Parables of the Dragnet and of the Householder." *Bibliotheca Sacra* 156 (1999) 282–96.
———. "The Parables of the Hidden Treasure and of the Pearl Merchant." *Bibliotheca Sacra* 156 (1999) 175–89.
———. "The Parable of the Leavening Process." *Bibliotheca Sacra* 156 (1999) 64, 61–71.
———. "The Parable of the Mustard Seed." *Bibliotheca Sacra* 155 (1998) 449–59.
———. "The Parable of the Sower and the Soils." *Bibliotheca Sacra* 155 (1998) 172–88.
Barclay, William. *The Acts of the Apostles*. Louisville: Westminster John Knox, 2017.
Beasley-Murray, George R. *Jesus and the Kingdom of God*. Grand Rapids, MI: Eerdmans, 1986.
Blomberg, Craig, L. *Interpreting the Parables*. Downers Grove, IL: Intervarsity, 1990.
———. *Matthew*. New American Commentary. Nashville: Broadman, 1992.
Buie, James. "'Me' Decades Generate Depression." *APA Monitor* (1991) 18.
Bunch, Morris A. *A Guide to Christian Ethics*. Eugene, OR: Wipf & Stock, 2013.
Bunyan, John. *The Pilgrim's Progress*. Orleans: Paraclete, 1992.
Condon, Bill, dir. *Mr. Holmes*. London: BBC Films, 2015.
Conzelmann, Hans. *Die Mitte der Zeit. Studien zur Theologie des Lukas*. Tübingen: Mohr-Siebeck, 1993.
De Saint Exupéry, Antoine. *The Little Prince*. New York: Mariner Books, 2000.
Dodd, Charles H. *The Parables of the Kingdom*. New York: Scribner & Sons, 1961.
Donahue, John R. *The Gospel in Parable*. Philadelphia: Fortress, 1988.
Emmrich, Martin. "The Temptation Narrative of Gen 3:1–6. A Prelude to the Pentateuch and the History of Pre-exilic Israel." *Evangelical Quarterly* 73 (2001) 3–20.

Bibliography

Fenton, John C. "The Parables of the Treasure and the Pearl (Matt. 13:44–46)." *Expository Times* 77 (1966) 178–79.
Freund, Christine. *Glücklich Mögest Du Wandern*. Wuppertal: Kiefel Verlag, 1992.
Gerhardsson, Birger. "The Seven Parables of Matthew 13." *New Testament Studies* 19 (1972) 16–37.
Green, Michael. *Matthew for Today*. Dallas: Word, 1988.
Hagner, Donald A. "Matthew's Parables of the Kingdom." In *The Challenge of Jesus' Parables*, edited by Richard N. Longenecker, 102–24. Grand Rapids, MI: Eerdmans, 2000.
———. *Matthew 1–13*. Dallas: Word, 1993.
Hill, David. *The Gospel of Matthew*. Grand Rapids, MI: Eerdmans, 1981.
Hultgren, Arland J. *The Parables of Jesus: A Commentary*. Grand Rapids. MI: Eerdmans, 2002.
Hunter, Archibald. *Interpreting the Parables*. Philadelphia: Westminster, 1960.
Jeremias, Joachim. *The Parables of Jesus*. Translated by Samuel H. Hooke. 2nd ed. New York: Scribner and Sons, 1954.
Kingsbury, Jack D. *Matthew 13: A Study in Redaction Criticism*. Richmond, VA: Knox, 1969.
Kistemaker, Simon, J. *The Parables of Jesus*. Grand Rapids, MI: Baker, 1980.
Køppen, Adolf Ludvig. *The World in the Middle Ages*. New York: Appleton, 1854.
Ladd, George E. *The Presence of the Future: The Eschatology of Biblical Realism*. Grand Rapids, MI: Eerdmans, 1974.
Lems, Shane. "On the Proper Use of Sickness (Pascal)." *The Reformed Reader*, May 13, 2019. https://reformedreader.wordpress.com/2019/05/13/on-the-proper-use-of-sickness-pascal/.
Lewis, C. S. *The Screwtape Letters*. New York: Macmillan, 1977.
McLaughlin, Rebecca. *Confronting Christianity: 12 Hard Questions for the World's Largest Religion*. Wheaton, IL: Crossway, 2019.
Mingren, Wu. "The Hoxne Hoard: How a Mislaid Hammer Led to the Largest Roman Treasure in Britain." *Ancient Origins*, August 4, 2018. https://www.ancient-origins.net/artifacts-other-artifacts/hoxne-hoard-0010494.
Morris, Leon. *The Gospel According to Matthew*. Grand Rapids, MI: Eerdmans, 1992.
Open Doors. "World Watch List." https://www.opendoorsusa.org/christian-persecution/world-watch-list/.
Payne, Philip B. "Jesus' Implicit Claim to Deity in His Parables." *Trinity Journal* 2 (1981) 2–23.
Pennington, T. Jonathan. "Matthew 13 and the Function of the Parables in the First Gospel." *Southern Baptist Journal of Theology* 13 (2009) 12–20.
Schlossberg, Herbert. *Idols for Destruction: The Conflict of Christian Faith and American Culture*. Wheaton, IL: Crossway, 1993.
Schnackenburg, Rudolf. *God's Rule and Kingdom*. Translated by John Murray. New York: Herder & Herder, 1963.

Bibliography

Senior, Donald. *Matthew*. Nashville: Abingdon, 1998.
Sider, John W. "Interpreting the Hid Treasure." *Christian Scholar's Review* 13 (1984) 360–72.
Snodgrass, Klyne. *Stories with Intent. A Comprehensive Guide to the Parables of Jesus*. Grand Rapids, MI: Eerdmans, 2008.
Stallard, Michael. "Hermeneutics and Matthew 13, Part II." *Conservative Theological Journal* 5 (2001) 324–59.
Stetson, B., and Joseph G. Conti. *The Truth about Tolerance*. Downers Grove, IL: Intervarsity, 2005.
Rezk, Tony. "Icon of the 21 martyrs of Libya!" Twitter, February 22, 2015, 10:06 a.m. https://twitter.com/tonyrezk/status/569558890305748992.
Teuffel, Jochen. "'Lasst uns der Welt antworten, wenn sie uns furchtsam machen will: Eure Herren gehen, unser Herr aber kommt!'—Gustav Heinemanns Rede auf dem Essener Kirchentag 1950 (vollständiger Text)." *NAMENSgedächtnis*, January 5, 2019. https://jochenteuffel.com/2019/01/05/lasst-uns-der-welt-antworten-wenn-sie-uns-furchtsam-machen-will-eure-herren-gehen-unser-herr-aber-kommt-gustav-heinemanns-rede-auf-dem-essener-kirchentag-1950-vollstaendiger-text/.
Thomson, A. John. *The Land and the Bible*. Grand Rapids, MI: Eerdmans, 1954.
Touissant, D. Stanley. *Behold Your King*. Portland, OR: Multnomah, 1980.
———. "The Introductory and Concluding Parables of Matthew Thirteen." *Bibliotheca Sacra* 121 (1964) 351–55.
Trench, Richard C. *Notes on the Parables of Our Lord*. Grand Rapids, MI: Baker, 1948.
Trinity Psalter Hymnal. Willow Grove, PA: Trinity Psalter Hymnal Joint Venture, 2018.
Walvoord, John F. *Matthew: Thy Kingdom Come*. Chicago: Moody, 1974.
Welch, T. Edward. *Depression: Looking Up from the Stubborn Darkness*. Greensboro, NC: Growth, 2004.
Wenham, David. *The Parables of Jesus*. London: Hodder & Stoughton, 1989.
Witherington, Ben, III. *Jesus the Sage: The Pilgrimage of Wisdom*. Minneapolis: Fortress, 2000.
Wright, T. Nicholas. *Jesus and the Victory of God*. Minneapolis: Fortress, 1996.
Young, Brad, H. *Jesus and His Jewish Parables*. New York: Paulist, 1989.
Zohary, Michael. *Plants of the Bible*. New York: Cambridge University Press, 1982.

www.ingramcontent.com/pod-product-compliance
Lightning Source LLC
Chambersburg PA
CBHW070932160426
43193CB00011B/1665